Pressing Toward the Mark

Pressing Toward the Mark

Christian Ethics for the Black Church Today

E. HAMMOND OGLESBY

Wipf & Stock
PUBLISHERS
Eugene, Oregon

PRESSING TOWARD THE MARK
Christian Ethics for the Black Church Today

Revised Standard Version of the Bible, copyright 1952 [2nd edition, 1971] by the
Division of Christian Education of the National Council of the Churches of Christ
in the United States of America. Used by permission. All rights reserved.

"Ode to the Southern Woman," reprinted with the permission of Benson Ebinne
and Rycraw Productions

ISBN 13: 978-1-4982-4920-1

Dedicated to
Jordan Christian, Trenton Alexander, and Derek William—
our grandsons—and to all sons and daughters
who are nurtured in faith.

A person without faith has no future.
—Michael J. Cheatham

Not that I have already obtained this or am already perfect;
but I press on to make it my own
because Christ Jesus has made me his own.
Brethren, I do not consider that I have made it my own;
but one thing I do, forgetting what lies behind
and straining forward to what lies ahead,
I press on toward the goal for the prize
of the upward call of God in Christ Jesus.
—Philippians 3:12–14

Contents

Preface

THE PRIMARY purpose of this book is to better understand the importance of Christian Ethics in the black church tradition. Christian ethics begins with Christian beliefs, practices, and principles—in light of their relevance to a particular religious-cultural and social context. It has been said and some believe that ethics is not simply a matter of logic and theory but life and struggle. One ingredient of a morally true life therefore, is the task of *digging*: the unending struggle on the part of ordinary people to explore, unmask, and discover meaning in life—since we cannot avoid moral tragedy.

The American novelist William Wells Brown once remarked: "*We are what we remember.*" For African American Christians, we remember the "moral tragedy" of *de jure* segregation and Jim Crowism in the length and breadth of American society. But even more importantly, we remember the power of a freeing and unfailing God, who took the fragments of our suffering and turned them into instruments of faith and power.

The shaping of the moral character, culture, spirituality, and identity of African Americans is critically tied into the tradition of the black Church. In one sense, this book, "*Pressing Toward the Mark*," is a narrative report card about a people who never lost faith in an understanding of God as a God of deliverance and justice. For African American Christians, faith is confidence in the awesome power and presence of God to do a "new thing" essentially revolved around one resounding word, "Freedom!" Seemingly in the early black church tradition, there is the notion that faith breaks the chains from life's dungeons.

Now in Chapter One of this book, "Christian Ethics and Roots of the Black Church," I attempt to demonstrate that we as ordinary people of faith become ethical not by *chance*, but by *choice*. Here the writer explores certain ethical principles inherent in the black church tradition. Perhaps one of the most fascinating sections of this chapter deals with the perceived role of the black preacher in the life of the African American community. For example: What is the role of the black preacher in regard to suffering and oppression in America? Has the image of the black preacher significantly changed, given the emergence of so-called mega-churches in contemporary society?

Is the black preacher today more visionary or villain, in the attempt to proclaim the gospel? Why do women—given church membership patterns—seem to occupy more seats in comfortable pews while men hold greater seats of power in black American pulpits? These are a few of the questions that ignited my passion while probing the ethical roots of the black church tradition.

My work in recent years, as a Christian ethicist and teacher of seminary and graduate students encouraged me to take a critical look at the importance of womanist ethics and feminist ethics in the life of the local congregation. It is my conviction that one of the neglected moral issues in the black church—as well as the Civil Rights movement of the mid-fifties and sixties—is the issue of sexism. Therefore, in Chapters Two and Three, respectively, "Lifting As We Climb," and "Womanist Ethics with a New Beat"—we examine the extraordinary lives of Mary McLeod Bethune, Rosa Parks, and Coretta Scott King. They are bold examples of insightful voices arising from the black church tradition. Yet their contributions—individually and collectively—can symbolize a powerful corrective to the structural sexism in the contemporary black church today. Sociologically, studies suggest that the average congregation in the black community is approximately seventy percent women among the regular membership.

Now in Chapter Four, "Pressing Toward the Mark," I was asking myself as well as the reader questions about a viable method of moral discourse that could speak—with clarity—to the on-going issues that African Americans and other people of color must confront in contemporary American society. While there are many crucial socio-ethical issues on the front burner of the black community, I have called attention to three dominant ones: (*a*) the AIDS epidemic, (*b*) the growing reality of the absence of youth and young adult participation in black church life; and (*c*) the continuing battle against racism in our society today. For practicing Christians, one of the important questions raised—metaphorically, considered—is this: "What's in your bucket?" To answer and engage conversation around this question, I have proposed to the reader a list of twelve "proverbial principles" or "moral laws" to have in your bucket as followers of Christ. In terms of the book's format, the reader will observe that each chapter ends with a case study. This format is intentional, in order to build more ethical dialogue, self-reflection, small group discussion, or the exploration biblical texts associated with each case.

Undoubtedly, the strength and excitement of writing this book for me is the practical inclusion of case studies. Although these cases are fictionalized, they reflect the actual circumstances of many people today. They add, I believe, an extra dimension to the process of ethical reflection and our treatment of the black church tradition in America. In any event, the "case method" itself offers an angle of vision and an invitation to cross-cultural dialogue that may open up new vistas of learning and self-understanding among women and men of faith—in response to the echoing sound within: I am *"Pressing Toward the Mark"* (Phil 3:12–14).

In the formative stages of my research, I am pleased to say that Mary Swehla and Caron Strother—administrative staff persons of Eden Theological Seminary—have provided me with valuable assistance in typing the earlier drafts of this book.

Finally, I wish to offer a special word of thanks to my wife, Gloria, who has reinforced for me—during the course of my own intellectual journey—the value of integrating ethnicity, faith, and identity. While on sabbatical leave from Eden Seminary in the Spring semester of 2006, I also owe a word of gratitude to President David Greenhaw and the faculty who gave me support and encouragement in the completion of my research project. Ultimately, my hope for you in reading this book is simple as it is spiritually awesome: that after reading this ethical essay you will be in a better relationship with Christ, our Risen Lord.

E. Hammond Oglesby

Chapter One

Christian Ethics
Roots of the Black Church

*In every human breast God has implanted a principle which we call
love of freedom; it is impatient of oppression, and pants for deliverance;
and by the leave of our modern Egyptians, I will assert that the same
principle lives in us.*

—Phillis Wheatley, 1753?–1784, Poet

*Freedom is a state of mind: a spiritual unchoking of the wells of human
power and super-human love.*

—W. E. B. DuBois, 1868–1963, Intellectual and Activist

Ethical Principles in Black Church Tradition

Christian ethics in the black church tradition begins with a love of Jesus as
Liberator and Provider. Basic Christian ethics in the black church tradition
starts with Jesus' own *revolutionary words* of the love of God and neighbor.
Jesus, as a Jew, made it clear for all who dared to listen that the attitude of
love is for all nations, all seasons, and moral traditions. As Liberator and
Provider, Jesus made it crystal clear the sorts of things which are morally
binding upon all humanity. For example, the New Testament ethical ethos
called it the "dual commandment." Accordingly, a Sadducee lawyer asked
Jesus a question—trying obviously to test and entrap him—and he gave
the perfect answer for all humanity to ponder:

> "Teacher, which is the great commandment in the law?" And he
> said to him, "You shall love the Lord your God with all your heart,
> and with all your soul, and with all your mind." This is the great

and first commandment. And a second is like it, "You shall love your neighbor as yourself" (Matt 22:36–40).

A vital presupposition of this ethical command is to remember that the attitude of love reflects the highest good for every individual, every interpersonal relationship, every family, every church community, and every nation in our global society. As humans, regardless of what race, creed, color, class, gender or sexual orientation, *we are never obligated not to love.* Jesus as Liberator and Provider, at every point in his own public ministry, demonstrated the importance of love for one another. Jesus as Liberator and Provider reminds us that love *covers your back* in good times as well as in bad. We are commanded, therefore, to reach out and love the other not only because "God is love" (1 John 4:16), but because the love of God itself will rise up inside of you and cast out the blindness in regard to my neighbor's or my brother's good. As Holy Scripture affirms: "And this commandment we have from him, that he who loves God should love his brother also" (1 John 4:21). For Jesus, our Liberator and Provider, the attitude of love is imperative not only for our own sanity—seemingly in a society gone mad—but also for the neighbor's good.

Furthermore, Christian ethics in the black church tradition affirms an understanding of the love of Jesus as Liberator and Provider, because the message of the gospel is the ground upon which we walk. As one faithful mother would often say (as I remember growing up as a child in the St. James Missionary Baptist Church of Earle, Arkansas) that "Jesus is my all and all . . . I can go to Him in prayer . . . for He knows my every care!" The love of Jesus as Liberator and Provider is the "true vine" that produces much fruit in the hearts, souls, and minds of people living in our troubled world (John 15:1–5). The love of Jesus is like the gentle eagle that stirs the nest, in order for the little ones to begin to fly, but under the ever-protective wings of the mother eagle. The love of Jesus as Liberator and Provider is like the deep roots of an old oak tree. Here I suspect, metaphorically, that when the storms of life come and forcefully beat upon the tree in a violent way, it may bend but it will not break the old oak tree because its roots are firmly anchored in the soil of God's mercy and righteousness. To be sure, Jesus gives to the downtrodden and hurting ones in our world deliverance from troubles and oppression (Ps 34:1–6).

Thus, the love of Jesus as Liberator and Provider is not about theological speculation concerning some abstract notion of the good and right thing to do. Rather, the moment you meet Jesus as Liberator or Savior, the good and the right come together as a new creation, a new being in Christ.

As we encounter Christ, we become new beings—set free from the chains that bind. As brothers and sisters in Christ, listen to the echo of freedom as witnessed in Holy Scripture:

> For freedom Christ has set us free; stand fast therefore, and do not submit again to a yoke of slavery. (Gal 5:1)

First of all, the motif of the *love of freedom* has always been a distinguishing characteristic of the black church tradition in America. Theologically, it is no accident that Jesus is perceived as Liberator and Provider in the hearts, souls, and minds of many African American Christians today. The historical circumstances of suffering and oppression put in the hearts of people of African descent a deep yearning for the fruit of freedom. It seems to me that fruit of freedom was implicitly and explicitly manifested in many of the religio-cultural traditions transmitted from Africa to New World societies in Brazil, the Caribbean, and North America.

For example, certain patterns of worship in the black church tradition, particular forms of communal praise, veneration of the ancestors, African-style drumming and dancing, rites of initiation from boyhood to manhood, and the use of sacred emblems as a sign of divine favor all reflect, to some degree, this preoccupation with a *love of freedom*. In a brilliant way, Albert J. Raboteau points out in his book *Slave Religion: The "Invisible Institution" in the Antebellum South*, that the iron hands of slavery and brutal oppression did not totally destroy the "moral core" and living African heritage of black people in the New World. Despite the continuing debate among historians, theologians, and religious leaders over the continuity or discontinuity of African religious tradition today, the good news is centered in a common claim of a love of freedom. Here freedom is not only an abstract by-product of the head, rather freedom is a passionate craving of the human heart. In terms of Christian ethics in the black church tradition, the love of freedom is a pivotal root that unlocks the wonders of God's wisdom and grace in a land where people of color have been victims of disgrace, slavery, and humiliation. Now in the historical circumstances of black suffering, I find it positively amusing how some slaves fought against the myth of black inferiority by simply thinking critically for themselves. Listen to this report and story by former slave "Aunt" Adeline in regard to a love of freedom:

> I had always been told from the time I was a small child that I was a Negro of African stock. That it was no disgrace to be a Negro and had it not been for the white folks who brought us over here from

Africa as slaves, we would never have been here and would have been much better off.[1]

As a follower of Jesus Christ, I strongly believe and affirm the love of freedom as a *root value* in our struggle to better understand the religio-cultural tradition of the black church in America. Theologically discerned, the love of freedom is a gift of God. God wills freedom for human creation. But it is a freedom bought with a price. Freedom is not free; it always involves personal responsibility as Christians. Too many people today who profess to be "Christian" are bound by the false assumption that we can know God without loving and knowing one another; that we want God without his passion for the poor and marginalized in the world; we want Christ without surrender and obedience; and we want love without sacrifice. The Christian moral life speaks a truth that must be inclusive of all of these elements. Certainly, oppressed slaves who embraced Christian faith knew, deep within, that when God took away their sins, they would find *deliverance* not simply in Heaven but here on Earth. Accordingly, the noted scholar Professor Eugene D. Genovese, in his classic volume *Roll, Jordan, Roll*, makes a cogently relevant observation regarding the world of slaves, vis-à-vis Christianity:

> However much the slaves, as Christians, felt the weight of sin, they resisted those perversions of doctrine, which would have made them feel unworthy as a people before God. Their Christianity strengthened their ties to their "white folks" but also strengthened their love for each other and their pride in being black people. And it gave them a firm yardstick with which to measure the behavior of their masters, to judge them, and to find them wanting. The slaves transformed the promise of personal redemption into a promise of deliverance as a people in this world as well as the next.[2]

In the second place, slaves, as Christians, were drawn to the ethical tenets of biblical faith not only because they held the conviction that "they loved Jesus" but also the realization that "God loves us." God's love for us empowers our being in human community. God's love for us, especially as a people with a shared memory of suffering and oppression, will not return void in the long struggle for freedom, justice, and racial equality in American society. Hence, the ethical principle of "God's love for us" points us toward the importance of *family love*. Christian ethics in the black church tradition affirms the crucial value of *family ties* and family love. There is, undoubtedly, a certain bond in the tapestry of family love that cannot be found in the solitary life of the individual. God loves us as individuals in need of grace—"Yes!" But even more dynamic, God seems to love us in the form of *family* as the universal expression of a covenant promise (Deut 7:6–9; John 3:16). The enduring symbol between God and the whole created order is covenant-love.

Ethically considered, this principle in the black church tradition means "family love." Therefore, it is my fundamental belief and observation that *family love* is a key principle in our struggle to understand the beauty and complexity of the black church tradition. Metaphorically, we can say that "God's love for us" is the root of the vine, and family love is a blossoming branch of the vine. As family, it is powerful to remember that in the theater of love God always takes the *first* step toward us. Simple as it is profound, every one of us who believes in Jesus as Liberator and Provider is morally obligated to respond in love to one's brother or sister. On this point the Bible clearly states: "We love, because He first loved us. If any one says 'I love God,' and hates his brother, he is a liar; for he who does not love his brother whom he has seen, cannot love God whom he has not seen" (1 John 4:19–20). Be that as it may, I am convinced in my own heart, mind, and spirit that the principle of "God's love for us" takes the functional expression—more often than not—of family love in the black church tradition. For example, in his classic book *A Black Political Theology*, J. Deotis Roberts discusses the fascinating paradigm *ujamaa*, which is an African concept meaning "family-hood" or "the love of family." In exploring the boundaries of social struggle in the black church tradition, in light of the radical love revealed in Jesus Christ, Roberts writes:

> Love as Jesus understood it is an urge for social cooperation in which the cooperating parties treat each other as persons. The welfare of the individual is furthered by the cooperation of all those who are members of the group. In order for an individual to be personal, he must act from within some group. Individuals are persons in society. The church as a fellowship should provide the climate for the flowering of that which is most truly personal as well as the manifestation of genuine community.[3]

In the third place, Christian ethics for and in the black church tradition seems to affirm that God favors the poor and marginalized in our world. The drama of God's unending love and presence with the people of Israel as disclosed in the Exodus story is a testimony to the freeing and unfailing power of the Creator. It seems to me that in the context of the black church tradition, there is a *feeling* and perception that the Exodus story is *our* story: that the particular thoughts, actions, images, and sufferings of the ancient Hebrew people are spiritually and emotionally connected to the experiences of slavery, moral degradation, and poverty heaped upon the shoulders of blacks and other people of color in America. Yet in spite of these forms of racial injustice and dehumanization, the God of the Bible still favors the poor, the least, and the last in our global community. If Christian ethics begins with Christian beliefs, then one of those scandalous beliefs is the story of God's love and presence with the needy and outcast. Therefore, the ethical concern for the poor and "disinherited" in the land is a constant refrain in the black church tradition. God loves us; but I don't think many of us actually comprehend how radical this love is in the moral struggle for justice in behalf of the poor. For example, in the book of the prophet Isaiah, there are burning "woe oracles" against the mistreatment of the needy. Notice this woe oracle in Isaiah 10:1–2:

> Woe to those who decree iniquitous decrees, and the writers who keep writing oppression, to turn aside the needy from justice and to rob the poor of my people of their right, that widows may be their spoil, and that they may make the fatherless their prey!

As an African American Christian ethicist, I find it interesting to note that the prophet Isaiah was not alone in condemning the sin and follies of injustice to the poor and needy. Jeremiah also cried out after the Babylonian exile of Judah (587 BC), seeking to make right what evil men had made wrong. Therefore, the prophet Jeremiah echoed a similar moral chorus as Isaiah:

> Wicked men are found among my people; they lurk like fowlers lying in wait. They set a trap; they catch men. Like a basket full of birds, their houses are full of treachery; therefore thy have become great and rich, they have grown fat and sleek. They know no bounds in deeds of wickedness; they judge not with justice the cause of the fatherless, to make it prosper, and they do not defend the rights of the needy. Shall I not punish them for these things? Says the Lord, and shall I not avenge myself on a nation such as this? (Jer 5:26–29)

In the fourth place, I suspect that Christian ethics in the black church tradition seems to affirm and echo the *principle of faith*. Of course, there is no simple and easy way to define faith in the context of contemporary black church life. For example, as an African American child growing up in Arkansas, I vividly remember how elders of the church would invariably quote from the popular biblical text Hebrews 11:1, which reads: "Now faith is the substance of things hoped for and the evidence of things not seen." I often pondered in the night what this biblical text could possibly mean through the eyes of a little child? Then, suddenly it occurred to me that as a youngster growing up in the southland, my mama would occasionally send me out to the collard greens patch near our house to fetch some fresh greens for the suppertime meal.

Now you see, brothers and sisters, my mama was a very good southern cook and she knew just how to fix those collard greens to sharpen one's appetite. In the recipe, she would add a measured amount of salt, pepper, garlic, onion, and a piece of "fat-back" (i.e., cured pork). Then mama would let the greens slowly cook in the pot for approximately two and one-half hours while baking a skillet of old fashioned corn bread in the oven. Now once the seven children in my immediate family had eagerly consumed the collard greens, one is left with the so-called "pot liquid." But if you are smart, you can take a piece of corn bread and still enjoy the pot liquid long after the greens are gone, because the *substance* is in the pot liquid! So it is with faith: faith is "the substance of things hoped for," symbolically, faith is the pot liquid readily providing substance and meaning to our lives.

Ethically discerned, the term "liquid" is derived from the Latin word *liquidus*, which means: "flowing smoothly and gracefully." This activity of readily flowing in God's will and purpose is connected, I think, with the essence of faith. While faith is a many-sided reality, it is purpose directed. Faith is goal-directed. In a manner of speaking, faith is what Christian ethicists today would call both *deontological and teleological.*[4] By this I mean to suggest that faith is concerned about one's "duty" to God, or the ultimate good in life. Symbolically, faith in the context of the black church tradition means keeping "our eyes on the prize," although the "prize" has not yet been fully won. Therefore, faith, on a deeper level of spirituality and moral consciousness, means "pressing toward the mark." Be that as it may, I fondly recall a country Baptist preacher, in the community of my childhood, speaking about the nature of faith. He quipped: "the faith that *fizzles* before the *finish* is faulty from the start."

For African American Christians, faith means many things to different people. For some the language of faith is a language of *reliance* upon God for the good and right thing to do in every social situation. Here faith is understood as basic trust in Almighty God, who admonishes us to do good at all times in the Christian moral life. Psalm 37:3 says: "Trust in the Lord, and do good; so you will dwell in the land, and enjoy security." The language of *reliance* sees faith-as-trust as he further declares: "Trust in the Lord with all your heart, and do not rely on your own insight. In all your ways acknowledge him, and he will make straight your paths" (Prov 3:5–6). For example, in the ethos of the black church tradition, there is a noted and charismatic preacher by the name of Rev. C. L. Franklin (1918–1984)—the father of the famous R & B singer Aretha Franklin—whose public ministry in our society has illustrated a notion of faith as *reliance* upon God. The language of faith as trust or *reliance* is crucial because it gives us strength for today and hope for tomorrow. As a servant of God, Rev. Franklin couched the issue of faith in the socio-historical context of his life's journey when he once remarked:

> As I reflect down the vistas of the past, as I think about all the problems and all the experiences I have had; without a faith in God, a faith in prayer, and a disposition of loyalty to God, I don't know what I would have done.[5]

While faith may be perceived as *reliance* or trust for some in the black church tradition, others view faith as essential for social struggle. Spiritually discerned, it may take the form of struggle existentially against sin, evil, and the wiles of Satan in our social situation. For example, it seems to me that the Apostle Paul articulated well the ethical burden and anguish of this internal struggle when he wrote:

> For I know that nothing good dwells within me, that is, in my flesh. I can will what is right, but I cannot do it. For I do not do the good I want, but the evil I do not want is what I do. Now if I do what I do not want, it is no longer I that do it, but sin which dwells within me. So I find it to be a law that when I want to right, evil lies close at hand. For I delight in the law of God, in my inmost self, but I see in my members another law at war with the law of my mind and making me captive to the law of sin which dwells in my members. Wretched man that I am! Who will deliver me from this body of death? Thanks be to God through Jesus Christ our Lord! So then, I of myself serve the law of God with my mind, but with my flesh I serve the law of sin. (Rom 7:18–25)

Christian ethics in the black church tradition seeks also to understand the language of faith as *social struggle*, in a political sense of what black people have had to suffer and endure as an oppressed minority, whose experiences have been shaped by the powerful influence of the institutionalized black church.

The very reality of social struggle invites African American Christians to reflect on the continuity between the black church and the critical needs in the black community. Social struggle challenges the ethically sensitive person to not only ponder a theoretical notion of the good and right thing to do, but to be aware of God's transforming spirit that speaks to us in *particular* and *universal* ways. In spite of the pressing issues and problems that divide African American Christians in contemporary society, the black church has been the primary institution that stood in the gap between destruction and survival, between vulnerability and virtue, and between despair and hope, as we seek to respond to the critical needs in the community. It has been said and some believe that social struggle is a moral good in and of itself. Ethically discerned, struggle is both internal and external. In the former, it is a necessary by-product of self-expression and self-initiative. In the latter, it is a collective by-product of self-determination and self-definition. Indeed, the language of social struggle suggests to the Christian believer that any people who want to be free have the right to determine their own destiny. Central to this collective endeavor in the African American community has been the presence of the black church that seems to preach a "universal message" of hope, forgiveness, freedom, and inclusion for all people. Professor C. Eric Lincoln makes this candid observation concerning the black church in regard to social struggle as he asserts:

> The black church, then, is in some sense a "universal church," claiming and representing all blacks out of a long tradition that looks back to the time when there was only the black church to bear witness to "who" or "what" a man was as he stood at the bar of his community. The church still accepts a broad-gauge responsibility for the black community inside and outside its formal communion. No one can die "outside the black church" if he is black.[6]

The vitality of social struggle is expressive of the black church in America. For example, it was the moral force behind the Civil Rights movement in the mid-1950s and early 1960s in our Democratic Republic. The insightful wisdom of an amazing civil rights chorus—the echoing voices of such icons as Thurgood Marshall, Rosa Parks, Martin Luther King, Jr., Coretta Scott King, Zora Neale Hurston, to name only a few—reminds us that struggle comes with a price. Just as freedom, as a visionary principle against the body politic of black suffering, is not free. So then, we as Christians are never free not to struggle for the common good. In short, I think that the abolitionist Frederick Douglass (1817–1895) put the language of faith as social struggle in a way that we all can constructively ponder:

> If there is no struggle, there is no progress. Those who profess to favor freedom, and yet deprecate agitation, are men who want crops

without plowing up the ground. They want rain without thunder and lightning. They want the ocean without the awful roar of its many waters. This struggle may be a moral one, or it may be a physical one, or it may be both moral and physical, but must be a struggle. Power concedes nothing without a demand.[7]

The Role of the Black Preacher: Visionary or Villain?

It has been said, and some believe, that the African American Church manifested across the historical or denominational spectrum, has been the most central social institution in shaping the lives and values of black people in America. As African American historians and theologians surveyed the cultural landscape of the mid-nineteenth century, there is no image or *personality* more dramatic than the black preacher. Historically discerned, scholars, and teachers of the Christian faith in the black church tradition have observed the unique role black preachers played in the life and culture of the community. Iconoclastic in breaking traditional beliefs held by the dominant culture in America, the role of the black preacher is both spiritual and moral. The dimension of the spiritual refers to the redeeming and living word of God. It is a way of saying, on a personal level, "Greater is He that is within me than is he that is in the world" (1 John 4). We can also find this reassuring affirmation of the dimension of the spiritual in Holy Scripture: "my God will supply all my needs according to His riches and glory" (Phil 4:19). In terms of role models in the black church tradition, the black preacher has been, seemingly, a persistent drum major for the spiritual. But the narrative story does not stop there. Metaphorically, the black preacher reflects a far more complex "personality type." Accordingly, W.E.B. DuBois provides this poetic description: "The Preacher is the most personality developed by the Negro on American soil. A leader, a politician, an orator, a 'boss,' an intriguer, an idealist—all these he is." Historically, the role of the black preacher as a unique personality in the struggle for freedom also incorporated a love of *virtue*. In the seminal volume, *In The Path of Virtue: the African American Moral Tradition*, Samuel K. Roberts boldly proclaims:

> African American race leaders reflected on the moral imperatives inherent in life in freedom after slavery. Both clerics and intellectuals were brought together in a common enterprise of discerning how black people could best secure a measure of social and moral

integrity in American life. Virtue could provide the undergirding structure for the total fabric of the responsible life.[8]

Concerning the status and esteem of which the black preacher was held among other professionals and educators in the community, Roberts further observes:

> At the same time, the black preacher was more than likely the most articulate person and, with other black professionals, among the better-educated people in the community, especially if the minister led a congregation of substantial size. By virtue of his position within the most central social institution in the black community, the black minister was bound to exert tremendous influence as one who could articulate issues concerning the destiny of the race.[9]

If the black church tradition, as we have argued consistently, is one of the chief sources through which the masses of the black race receive ethical guidance, the black preacher, then, is its principal actor in the drama of religious life. Just as the black church as a whole became the center of social, moral, and spiritual growth among black people, on the one hand; the black preacher eventually became the chief moral teacher and theological interpreter of the black religious experience, on the other. The black preacher, in no small way, exerts a dominant influence in the lives of the masses of black folk.[10]

In Carter G. Woodson's study of black religious life in America, particularly in his work *The History of the Negro Church*, the observation is made that the black preacher was not only the key actor who occupied the prestigious position of community leader and orator but moral spokesman as well. As moral spokesman, the black preacher was that individual, perhaps more than any other, who inspired a persecuted people to "think and to think on their feet," to express themselves in such a manner that enhanced dignity and self-respect among all persons in human community.[11] E. Franklin Frazier reminds us that it was the black preacher, during the pre-Civil War period of American history, who gave moral and religious instruction to his enslaved brothers and sisters. He accomplished this important task in spite of the perennial external threats to his own life, primarily through the medium of sermons, and the force of his own personal life as an example. But that was the black church of *history*. What about the "flavor" of the contemporary black church?

Although we have seen the positive role of the black preacher in *history*, in light of the rich spiritual and moral roots of the black church tradition, the critical question remains in contemporary society: Is the black preacher today largely perceived as a *visionary* or *villain* in proclaiming the word of God? I suspect that the question itself is ethically daunting and one that cries out for pragmatic response. Certainly, the roots of the black church tradition and its ideals of such elements as (*a*) love of freedom; (*b*) love of justice; (*c*) love of family; and (*d*) God's love for us, clearly speak for themselves.

Given the long view of history, these ideals have helped to sustain African American Christians and provided what Aretha Franklin—in her soulful gospel music—called "*A Bridge Over Troubled Water.*" Here the experiences and struggles of many reflect a communal testimony in such spirit filled phrases as "Jesus is my all and all!"; "I can go to Him in prayer, for he knows my every care!"; "I was out upon the stormy sea, but along came Jesus and rescued me!"; and "While I'm trying to figure it out, God has already worked it out!" Of course, the flavor of these poetic and communal testimonies go on and on in the corpus of the black church tradition and its music.

But are these life-giving stories and testimonies about God, Jesus Christ, the church, and moral struggle being lost from one generation to another? Who are the "keepers" and drum majors for the African American moral tradition today? Who or what will stand in the gap between sin and salvation? Who or what will stand in the gap between a growing drug culture among America's youths and America's dreamers for a better tomorrow? Who or what will stand in the gap between *violence* and *vision* in black urban America? Who or what will stand in the gap between the virtue of education and the vice of *mis-education* in the market place of our global economy? When will black people stop referring to one another as "niggers"? Have we forgotten that there will be no "niggers" in *Heaven*, only the righteous around God's throne? When will the dawn of wisdom, given to us by our African ancestors, appear and put new oil into our lamps? Will the role of the black preacher in American society today follow the path of a villain or visionary?

I strongly believe and think that every person who sits in the pew for Sunday morning worship, every Christian educator, every council president, every deacon, every choir member, and every youth participant in church life must openly and honestly probe the meaning of these questions as followers of Christ. From an ethical conceptual framework, the whole matter can be objectively put: Is the black preacher as pastor essentially a visionary or villain? Now in responding to the most urgent question, I wish to propose a more pragmatic indicator as a guide in the contemporary black church community. Since Jesus had twelve original disciples, I am going to give you twelve brief "scenarios" or critical issues for study and small group discussion. Therefore, people of faith need to think critically about the contrasting paths of a "visionary" versus a "villain." Consider the following for moral deliberation and action:

1. One elderly mother of the congregation muttered to another: "I've been a member of this church for over 40 years . . . and I have seen some good ministers come and go; but too many preachers today seem more concerned about driving big cars than the cure of souls . . . " What must we do? (See Rom 5:3–5)

2. "I don't feel spiritually fulfilled in my church anymore," said Peggy Harris, age 36, to her best friend Joan Gordon, age 34. She went on to quip, "I don't think it's all my fault either. The preaching of the word ain't what it used to be . . . I hear more today about a *gospel of prosperity* and less about a gospel of the Prince of Peace." Why is that? (See Matt 5:9)

3. "In my own faith community, we spend more money on church parking lots . . . than on church mission," complained one person who regularly attends Sunday morning worship. What would Jesus say about this? (See Matt 28:18–20)

4. "I like to visit mega churches," said Tom to his buddy Henry, "for the lively music . . . shouting, handclapping, and mega-praise . . . but I don't see many ministries of mega-justice for the downtrodden and needy in our world." What ought we to say or do? (See Matt 15:8–9)

5. Who is the visionary or villain . . . when the thirsty did not receive a cup of water . . . when the hungry were not fed; when the prisoner's hands and heart remain . . . untouched by the preacher; and when our children are abused and left alone on the mean streets in society? What is the role of ordinary Christians in confronting these circumstances? (See Matt 25:36–44, 19:14)

6. Who is the visionary or villain . . . when we continue to use the '*N*-word' on *ourselves* in the first decade of the twenty-first century, while fiercely denouncing the '*N*-word' as white people used it on us in the first decade of twentieth-century America. Who's fooling whom? ". . . there is something scary about looking at my own face in the mirror," said one black man to another. (See Acts 11:1–18)

7. "Preachers today are more concerned about *money* than *ministry*," said Sister Anderson, a faithful mother of the church." Did Jesus not intend for all to be saved and to put thy enemies under thy feet?" (See Matt 22:41–45)

8. "What's wrong with the church today is that we spend more time putting the preacher on a *pedestal*, than putting the gospel in the people," explained one critic of the contemporary black church. Is there any truth to this criticism? (See Matt 11:5, 9:35)

9. Visionary or villain? "Put God first so you won't have to worry about the 'second' or 'third' thing on the journey of life." (See Matt 6:33)

10. Sally ran up to her close friend Robyn at their regular Bible study meeting and said: "Girl . . . I recently found out a big secret in our small congregation . . . that two young women in our flock are lesbian lovers . . . but the pastor, I understand, wanna show compassion and keep them in the church . . . but I think they should be put out of the church, because this behavior is wrong . . . after all, they are not setting a good example for our young people." What will Robyn say? (See John 3:16)

11. Visionary or villain? "Do what you can to make a difference in the world, and let it go as we fight against the wiles of the devil?" (See Luke 22:31)

12. Visionary or villain? "Practice the art of humility and friendship as people of faith . . . stop walking passed each other and not speaking to one another as persons-in-community." (See John 15:15; Luke 15:6; Matt 11:19).

Keeping It Real:
The Landscape of Ethics in Society

So far in our discussion, we have already explored some of the roots, presuppositions, and sources for understanding Christian ethics in the black church tradition. Now it is imperative that we look at a functional perspective on the nature of ethics itself, its landscape, and its implications for a better life in society. There is an old Scottish proverb that says: "Ethics is not something that you think up in your head, but what you do through your heart." In a nutshell, the language of ethics in the African American Church tradition challenges us to "keep it real," to "hold on to God's unchanging hand," to "hold on not to the pain but the divine promises," and to "press toward the mark" as individual members of the body of Christ. Therefore, the language of ethics in the black experience for many people is never fully separated from the reality of the gospel of Jesus Christ in modern society.

Analytically, there appears to be no profound separation in the black religious community between the *profane* and *sacred*. Ethically, many Christian believers simply affirm, as a sign of obedience and trust, a functional perspective that tends to be expressed in such phrases as "God got the whole world in His hands," "God woke me up this morning and started me on my way," or "While I'm trying to figure it out, Jesus has already worked it out!" In the context of ethical discourse, these sorts of wisdom-filled "tidbits" have been a vital part of the *oral tradition* of the black church for many decades. They say something not simply about *whose* we are as Christians, but *where* we have come, in light of climbing the rough side of the mountain, and *pressing toward the mark* in American society. But still, given the moral problems of our time, we must ask the critical question: What is ethics?

Here we may simply define ethics as the critical study of morality. It is a process of self-critical reflection about the choices we make, and how they impact our values, faith, and conduct. In a classical sense, ethicists begin by raising the question: What ought I to do? Each human being is a moral agent as well as a child of God. Therefore, the moral agent seeks to understand what "ought to be," in light of "what is" in our society today. In our struggle to keep it real, ethics deals with a process of reasoning in regard to a criterion for what is right and wrong. Undoubtedly, the perennial ethical problematic is this: we usually, as humans, do not become that concerned, apparently, about what is right or wrong until our *rights* have been wronged!

In the sort of world in which we live, Christians and secular persons are concerned about issues and *rights* that confront us all. At nearly every junction of human life we are engaged in constant decision-making. We are creatures that practice the art of moral choice, whether we do this with intentionality or in a sporadic way. From the crack of dawn to the dusk of dark the human being is engaged in some form of ethical discourse.

In the first place, the term "ethics" is derived from the Greek word *ethos*, and the Latin *mos*. The former refers to a stall or dwelling. The latter means custom or usage as prescribed by the moral practices of a given community or society. Symbolically *ethos* is the cement that holds together community, in some sense of what is right and wrong conduct. Good conduct or fairness is the basis upon which community and society rest.

The Christian usage for "good manners" or "good conduct" is Jesus Christ himself as norm for the moral life. This thought is expressed, in part, by the moral directive set forth in the teachings of Jesus: "I am the way," said Jesus. "Follow me," said Jesus on another account, "and I will make you fishers of men" (Matt 9:9, 16:24). In each instance, the "way of life" of the gospel is expressive of what Christians and secular persons are commanded to do and be, in regard to the least among us. This is to say that there is, in the context of ethical thinking, a moral directive by which persons are obliged to follow an appropriate pattern of conduct, as a manner of life, which leads to a sense of goodness, maturity, and holiness on the part of the community of faith. Therefore, the word ethics is used to designate a way of life that is in conformity to the gospel of Jesus Christ and to the will of God. In whatever biblical field of study, the concerns of ethics are crucial because they raise the issues of what is right and good in individual behavior, in light of God's will for our lives.

In the second place, the word "ethics," in a functional sense, demands that we "keep it real" because it is not only concerned with a "way of life" in conformity to the will of God, but also with the process of decision-making and action. As such, the process must be consistent and relevant to the peculiar character of the Christian moral life as we go about arriving at the *right decision* on specific questions that we confront. Here the ethically sensitive person is concerned primarily with the systematic steps involved in the process of decision-making itself as to what constitutes appropriate and right action. For example, I will ask you to reflect on a "case study" at the end of this chapter, in terms of right action. To be sure, the Christian ethic seeks to discern those values and norms that guide us in making moral decisions. One appropriate step is *clarification* of the principles by which we live, move, and relate to others in human community. Another step in the process is that of *interpretation* of the life of Christians; for instance, what does it mean to be Christian in a society of conflicting values? Or what normative principle do we use to aid us in moral action? Perhaps another step in the complex process of decision-making and action is the concern by us all for the consequences of a particular course of moral action.

In the third place in our effort to keep it real, it is important to recognize that Christian ethics is strongly related to theology. Indeed, the very nature of Christian ethics is its awareness of a transcendent God. It is a vital part of theology in that it seeks to probe the ultimate meaning of particular moral action.

Here there is the assumption that one cannot adequately engage in Christian ethics apart from theology. Accordingly, ethics and theology are inseparable. Each needs the other in pondering such doctrines as creation and redemption, sin and atonement, promise and fulfillment, and liberation and reconciliation in the body of Christ. Neither Christian ethics nor theology will tolerate easy answers to these earthen and ultimate questions that Christians in the contemporary black church are bound to face. Thus if theology is concerned with the ultimate questions of creation and God's relation to the world, ethics is, then, the attempt to interpret how we decide and act in light of divine claims and God's redemptive love among us. So then, the upshot of this is, formally speaking, the threefold concern of ethics: the analysis of *ethos*, *clarification* and *interpretation* of principles undergirding moral behavior, and the question of an ultimate or transcendent reference point for right decisions and action. However, we also note that principles for decision-making are very seldom thought through with precision and clarity using a method that is relevant to the social condition.

Of course, for many people in contemporary society, happiness is the goal of the ethical life. Some of the core values that we as moral agents struggle with are the questions: Who am I? or What is my purpose in life?, *or* theologically, we tend to raise the penultimate question of faith, namely: What will God have me *do* or *be*? Moral agents are also concerned in the field of Christian social ethics with the interface of the "spoken word" in the Bible and human behavior in society. For example, what constitutes a good society? What marks represent right behavior? Without doubt, these are some of the pivotal questions and concerns inherent in the landscape of ethical discourse. For instance, the question of the relationship between "word and deed" is an old problematic of biblical ethics. We are admonished in the biblical material: "be not bearers of the word only, but doers" (Jas 1:22). The burden of ethics in both church and society involves being doers of the living word of God. For example, the black church tradition affirms the basic contention that biblical principles of faith must impact and transform human *conduct*. It seems to me, therefore, that this is the fundamental ethical lesson behind Romans 12:1–2:

> I appeal to you therefore, brothers and sisters, by the mercies of God, to present your bodies as a living sacrifice, holy and acceptable to God, which is your spiritual worship. Do not be conformed to this world, but be transformed by the renewing of your minds, so that you may discern what is the will of God—what is good and acceptable and perfect.

In understanding the landscape of ethics, this particular text is rich as a source for critical reflection. In the historical context, Paul was writing to the church at Rome, and he admonished the followers of Jesus Christ to remember their *calling*. Consider these marks upon the ethical landscape:

Vocational Calling as a Useful Source of Ethics.

Every Christian has a calling. The nineteenth-century novelist and poet William Wells Brown once remarked: "We are what we remember." As moral agents of the cross of Jesus Christ, remember the experiences and struggles that brought you thus far. Remember the particular story or *nudging* of the divine hand upon your life that inspired you to become a Christian. Remember from where it is God brought you. Remember your baptism. Remember the courage of your ancestors. This ethical text suggests that you, as brothers and sisters in Christ, "present your bodies as a living sacrifice, holy and acceptable to God" (Rom 12:1). It seems to me that this is an awesome ethical mandate for the people of God.

The Posture of the Transformed Non-Conformist.

This particular insight and "use" of ethics arises from the writings of the ethical theologian Martin Luther King, Jr., in his classic book, *Where Do We Go From Here: Chaos or Community?* Here King sets the stage for us to understand what it means to be a "transformed non-conformist" in the course of human affairs. In the flux of everyday life, people will often dump on you, deceive you, and abuse you verbally, physically, emotionally, or sexually in the name of their own twisted value system. Yet the values of Holy Scripture remind us to "be not conformed to the values of this world" (Rom 12:2). The ethical landscape of Holy Scripture reminds us to put our absolute trust in God, and not in the princes and cultural custodians of this present social order. Listen to the moral echo of the psalmist declaring:

> Put not your trust in Princes, in mortals, in whom there is no help. When their breathe departs, they return to the earth; on that very day their plans perish. Happy are those whose help is the God of Jacob; whose hope is in the Lord, who made heaven and earth . . . who keeps faith forever; who exercises justice for the oppressed; who gives food to the hungry. . . . The Lord loves the righteous; the Lord watches over the strangers. (Ps 146:1–9cf)

God Favors the Vulnerable and the Oppressed.

It is my passionate conviction that the landscape of ethics involves God's favor upon the most vulnerable and hurting ones among us in human society. Historically, the black church has always stood with and for the interests of the poor. There appears to be in Holy Scripture a moral predisposition to the poor and the oppressed in the sort of troubled world in which we live. Perhaps the classic example of this motif in the landscape of ethics can be seen in the way Jesus of Nazareth went about inaugurating his own ministry. The evangelist Luke recorded Jesus as saying, based on the prophet Isaiah as he unrolled the scroll and read:

> The Spirit of the hand is upon me, because he has anointed me to bring good news to the poor. He has sent me to proclaim release to the captives and the recovery of sight to the blind; to let the oppressed go free, to proclaim the year of God's favor. (Luke 4:18–19cf)

The motif of the "Lord's favor" toward the poor and the oppressed is a central theme in the landscape of ethics. A cursory glance into contemporary history would suggest that this ethical motif is present in a wide range of perspectives implicit in biblical theology, liberation theology, black theology, feminist theology, and womanist theology, and manifested in the lives of those scholars and writers who share a common memory of suffering and hope. The decisive ethical norm is this: God favors the outcast and the stranger, the poor and marginalized, and those who seek to do righteousness at all times (Acts 11:1–18). To be sure, the motif of the Lord's favor turns out to be a persistent and dominant theme inherent in the way we attempt to understand the critical norms of the landscape of ethics. Some informing perspectives and interpretations may include the following books: *Character is Destiny: The Value of Personal Ethics in Everyday Life*, by Russell W. Gough; *Lanterns: A Memoir of Mentors*, by Marian Wright Edelman; *Margins and Mainstreams: Asians in American History and Culture*, by Gary Y. Okiniko; *A Dream Unfinished: Theological Reflections on America from the Margins*, by Eleazar S. Fernandez, et. al.; and *Soul Survivors: An African American Spirituality*, by Carlyle Fielding Stewart III.

Love is Justice Distributed.

One of the difficult and perennial themes on the landscape of ethics is the relationship between love and justice in the biblical text. At times these deep moral themes appear to be separate; at other times they appear to be woven together. Whether ethicists and biblical scholars see them as interconnected or mutually exclusive should not defer our discernment of their crucial importance in Christian ethics. Of course, the classic example of the principle of justice in the Old Testament can be symbolized in the prophet Amos. The false piety of those who neglected the poor and hurting ones was found morally disgusting to God. Amos declared:

> I hate, I despise your feasts, and I take no delight in your solemn assemblies. Even though you offer me your burnt offerings . . . I will not accept them, and the peace offerings of your fatted beasts I will not look upon. Take away from me the noise of your songs; toe the melody of our harps, I will not listen. But let justice roll down like waters, and righteousness like an everflowing stream. (Amos 5:21–24cf)

In one's reflection upon the landscape of ethics, the basic conviction I wish to get over to you in this particular chapter arises from the fact that love and justice belong together. They are not mutually exclusive. I think that the "great error" in judgment of teaching and preaching among many pastors and leaders in the contemporary black church today arises from the fact that these two normative principles are too often kept separate in dealing with the conflicted issues and problems of our world. There can be no genuine love without justice in community; by the same token, there can be no genuine community without love. Now in our closing reflections on the landscape of ethics in the black church tradition, as well as the wider society, I wish to invite the reader to consider and discuss the following case.[12]

Case Study: After Katrina, Then What?

"Help me, please help me . . . I wanna go home; I don't want to eat this government food . . . I just want to eat my own food . . . I wanna go home!" This was the desperate cry of an African American woman, echoed on the national news media in the wake of destruction left behind by Hurricane Katrina during the last week in August 2005. Some initially called her a *refugee*—a dreaded word to be used in American democracy against its own citizens.

Ethically, I strongly believe that Katrina was a wake-up call for our nation, our churches, our multicultural communities of faith, and all people who love life, freedom, and the safety of our children in a democratic society. In terms of national security and the future safety of our children, in particular, social psychologists and philosophers remind us—given the demands of parenting in a healthy family environment—that we tend to give our children three things: (*a*) *protection*; (*b*) *permission*, that is to say "a sense of right and wrong and where the moral boundaries are located in social behavior"; and (*c*) *potency*, that is to say "a sense of self-reliance, confidence, and responsibility to take their little *wings* and fly." As a theologian, I suggest that as we confront the uncertainties and pains of life, we must add one other "*p*" and that is the power of *prayer*. Many of the survivors, for example, I've had the privilege of meeting, largely at churches throughout America, told me that: "If it had not been for prayer . . . and a feeling of God's presence on my side . . . I would not have survived the raging flood waters." Of course, many were not so fortunate as to live to tell their stories.

Unfortunately, in the Katrina disaster, recent studies show that at least 80% of the people in the city of New Orleans lost their homes. The toll on human life was nearly 1,700 dead, and 20,000 people missing. Ray Nagin, Mayor of New Orleans, reported to our nation that approximately half of African American residents living in the city lost everything they owned. A few days after the massive storm, one local leader lamented: "Katrina exposed poverty in urban America and the politics of neglect . . . this is a living hell . . . beyond anything Satan could cook up." Although the federal government has appropriated 87 billion dollars for assistance in rebuilding, less than half of the people have returned. Amazingly, Helen has a different attitude despite the fact that she is unsure about her future.

The main character of this story, Helen, is 55 years old and the proud mother of six children and four grandchildren. She comes from a working class family and has lived in New Orleans for most of her life. Like many other people from the class of the working poor, Helen carved out a job for herself in the tourism industry of New Orleans, moving up the socio-economic ladder from maid to manager of maid services at a local prestigious hotel. Helen never thought, in her wildest dreams, that something like Katrina—a category four storm—would ever happen to her community! Trying to make sense from her shattered life, Helen mused within her soul these daunting questions: Who is to blame for the apparently slow response time by the Federal Emergency Management Agency (FEMA), the U. S. Government, the National Guard, and some church organizations? Can the church lead the society in social rituals of what it means to show justice, mercy, and compassion to the victimized and hurting ones (Mic 6:8)?

Theologically, Helen and many other victims wonder if this tragic event was simply another natural disaster in the course of Mother Nature—viewed through our liberal enlightenment lens—or is God trying to get our attention, as in the days of Noah and the groaning of creation? What sorts of issues are raised for the church and its mission? What constitutes a faithful response in this devastating aftermath of Katrina? What is the most loving thing to do in light of Helen's concrete situation? As the curtain falls down on this story, Helen hardly knows which way to turn. She is destitute and without a job because her place of employment has suffered tremendous water damage. Be that as it may, survival relief is one thing, but Helen wants to go home—if there is a home to go to—so she can re-build a broken life. O Lord, is anybody listening to the nameless "Helens" who roam the flood zones seeking shelter from the incomprehensible storms of life? As a caring person, what am I, as a believer in Jesus Christ and a member of his church, to do?

Ethical Approach

1. What would be a responsible approach to this case?

2. Identify and discuss your mixed feelings about people who were trapped—some on rooftops—by the flood?

3. What would Jesus likely say or do?

Issues for Study and Discussion

1. In what ways do you identify with the pain and frustration Helen is going through? (See Gal 6:2; Heb. 9:28; Jas 2:14–18)

2. What is the role of our federal government, in light of such a massive disaster in our land? (See Amos 5:22–24; Luke 12:24–27; John 21:16)

3. What lessons have we learned from Katrina that could possibly impact our national security in the future? (See Mic 6:8)

4. Was race or ethnicity a factor in the speed of the relief effort in responding to the Katrina crisis? (See Gal 3:28–29; Acts 11:1–18)

5. Who among us are morally charged and responsible for speaking the truth in love? (See Eph 4:14–16, 25–29; Phil 3:2–4)

6. If you were President of the United States, how would you likely use your authoritative powers to *prevent* another Katrina? (See Prov 8:1–9, 12:1–3; Isa 26:7–11; Ps 63:1–9)

Notes

1. Albert J. Raboteau, *Slave Religion: The Invisible Institution in the Antebellum South* (New York: Oxford University Press, 1978, 2004) 43. In the critical discussion and debate over the role of slave religion in the deep antebellum south, there was little doubt among believers that it served as a source of strength for sojourners, and as a tool of survival for a people who had been psychologically and physically snatched from the security of their African homeland and brought to a strange world, under the yoke of oppression. Despite the pain of physical exploitation in slavery, the reality of "slave religion" gave to slaves themselves a sense of worth before God. Accordingly, the noted historian Eugene D. Genovese puts it this way: "The religion practiced in quarters gave slaves the one thing they absolutely had to have if they were to resist being transformed into the Sambos they had been programmed to become. It fired them with a sense of their own worth before God and man. It enabled them to prove to themselves, and to a world that never ceased to need reminding, that no man's will can become that of another unless he himself wills it—that the ideal of slavery cannot be realized, no matter how badly the body is broken and the spirit tormented." (Eugene D. Genovese, *Roll, Jordan, Roll,* New York: Vintage Books, 1974) 283.

2. Eugene D. Genovese, *Roll, Jordan, Roll: The World The Slaves Made* (New York: Vintage Books, 1974) 283.

3. J. Deotis Roberts, *A Black Political Theology* (Philadelphia: Westminster Press, 1974) 166. It is important for us to note that in the context of the African American moral tradition, the idea of "family love" is a by-product of Ancient African Culture—where a mother or father would name the child to reflect a certain experience or value. For example, "if the birth occurs during rain," says John S. Mbiti, "the child would be given a name which means 'Rain,' or 'Rainy,' 'Water,' if the mother is on a journey at the time, the child might be called 'Traveler,' 'Stranger' . . . , Wanderer . . . ." Rhetorically, the notion of family love would never take the form of naming a child in such a way that would hurt the child's self-identity—with such labels as "nigger," "lazybone," "little Sambo," or "darkie." In the language of Swahili, for instance, names such as Tai (meaning "Eagle"), Msiter (meaning "Forest"), or Mlima (meaning "Mountain") may be regarded as positive expressions of family love in certain religio-cultural traditions of East Africa. Therefore, it is not insignificant for us to recognize the moral link between family love and the ritual of naming our children—that reflect some pattern of meaning. (See John S. Mbiti, *African Religions and Philosophies*, New York: Anchor Books, 1970, 154.)

4. Lisa Soule Cahill and James F. Childress, eds., *Christian Ethics: Problems and Prospects* (Cleveland: The Pilgrim Press, 1996) 210–211. For Christian believers, the critical process of reflection may take the form of both *teleological* and *deontological* reasoning. Ethicists and theologians often refer to two normative rules of thumb that people of faith appeal to in conflicted situations. One rule of thumb can be understood as the "ethics of aspiration" (i.e., teleological), which tends to be goal-oriented. Hence, it is concerned primarily with the *telos* or the "end" of human behavior. The other rule of thumb can be understood as the "ethics of obligation," which implies a sense of moral commitment or "duty" in regard to a particular course of action. For example, when the moral question concerning the obligation to "forgive" was raised, the gospel tradition of Jesus was decisive and crystal clear in its response (Matt 6:14, 18:35; Luke 6:37). Historically, we may also note the

functionality of the "ethics of obligation" in the life of nineteenth-century abolitionist Frederick Douglass who strongly believed that it was ethically plausible that slaves work for their own freedom. They had, absolutely, an obligation to do so, given the situation of oppression imposed by the power brokers of white southern society. As such, slaves were both *rule-deontologists* and *rule-teleologists* in their persistent moral struggle to make freedom a reality. To be sure, these material moral norms implicit in "teleology" and "deontology" are illuminative elements of what ought to be—as African American Christians attempt to make sense out of the meaning of black suffering in the world.

5. Richard Newman, *African American Quotations* (New York: Checkmark Books, 2000) 137.

6. Cited in Preston Robert Washington, *God's Transforming Spirit: Black Church Renewal* (Valley Forge: Judson Press, 1988) 20.

7. Newman, 346–347.

8. Samuel K. Roberts, *In The Path of Virtue: The African American Moral Tradition* (Cleveland: The Pilgrim Press, 1999) 108. The notion that "knowledge is virtue" is deeply interwoven into the fabric of the black church tradition. Hence, both clerics and intellectuals nurtured the interplay of religion and education in the social struggle of people of African descent. For Roberts, virtue is expressive of freedom, human dignity, and the search for the "good" inherent in the African American moral tradition. Like the philosophers of ancient Greek culture, the search for the good and that which reflects "virtue" involves self-examination in every day life. For example, Socrates, at his trial in 399 B. C., maintained that the reason he philosophized was that "the unexamined life was not worth living." Therefore, the language of "virtue" asks: "What is the good life for all people?" In nineteenth-century America, the slaves boldly responded: "Freedom!" "Freedom!" "Freedom!"

9. Ibid.

10. Enoch H. Oglesby, *Ethics and Theology From The Other Side: Sounds of Moral Struggle* (Washington D.C.: University Press of America, Inc., 1979) 35.

11. Ibid., 36.

12. "Case study: *After Katrina, Then What?*" I wrote this particular case shortly after our nation had experienced one of the worst natural disasters in U.S. history. It is only a glimpse into the obvious to suggest that ordinary people of goodwill have responded by the millions to people victimized by this epical tragedy. As case readers, our pragmatic task involves a critical investigation and ethical discussion on the issues at stake for both Church and society. Ultimately, we must ponder the question: What is the role of Christians for the black church and beyond, in terms of *preventing* another "Katrina disaster?" As American citizens of goodwill, *what ought we to do?*

Chapter Two

Lifting as We Climb
The Story of Mary McLeod Bethune

Who can find a virtuous woman?
For her worth is far beyond coral.
—Proverbs 31:10

No person is your friend who demands your silence,
or denies your right to grow.
—Alice Walker, 1944–
Acclaimed Author and Activist

MARY MCLEOD Bethune was one of the most dynamic and revolutionary leaders of the twentieth century, and her thought has been interpreted in many diverse ways. Feminist and womanist theologians have lauded her as a "black Moses" for her people at a time when traditional American values limited the role of women to home and family life. By the way, we shall examine more carefully the "womanist" or "feminist" outlook in the next chapter. Some have lifted up her quiet defiance of ruthless segregation laws and oppressive Jim Crowism as a sign of a social prophet. Other writers have noted her extraordinary leadership ability in matters of education, human rights, and political diplomacy at a peculiar time in American history when the dominant culture was trying to "make the world safe for democracy," while blatantly denying democracy and justice to its own citizens of color.

There have been many fine expositions of her intellectual genius as an educator and administrator. For example, the recent and critically acclaimed volume by Professor Sheila Y. Flemming, *The Answered Prayer to a Dream: Bethune-Cookman College 1904–1994*, is a case in point. The emphasis here, however, will be on her moral teachings and spirituality as a disciplined thinker and renowned theological educator. While she actively participated in public life—involving presidents, kings, foreign heads of nations, and professional organizations in the global society—she remained a person of prayer and spiritual centeredness who anchored her progressive faith in a God of justice and love for the downtrodden. To paraphrase Alice Walker, it may be said that Mary McLeod Bethune morally resisted any person who "demanded her silence, or denied her the right to grow." Now in terms of a negative imperative, we may put the matter proverbially: "If you make yourself a doormat, people will wipe their feet on you." Well, it is only a glimpse into the obvious to suggest that Mary McLeod Bethune never allowed anyone to wipe their feet on her, despite the degradation of racial bigotry and *de jure* ("by law") *segregation*. Logically and morally, we are compelled to ponder the question: Who was Mary McLeod Bethune?

Early Testimonies: "She's Different, She's a Child of Prayer"

The testimony of the midwife who delivered her into this world is vividly striking: "She came with her eyes wide open. She'll see things before they happen."[1] Testimony *per se*, has always had a high place of esteem in the troubling waters of the black experience in America. The language of "testimony" itself is borrowed from the world of courtroom trials, in which the judge and the jury attempt to sort out, as they carefully hear, conflicting claims to the truth. The language of testimony is a form of community speech that seeks to bear witness to the truth as ordinary people share, respond, and experience it within the socio-religious arena of life. Therefore, the testimony of the midwife was indicative of the fact that something very significant has happened in the birth of this child: Mary Jane McLeod. Through the gift of moral discernment, this peculiar child, dark and lovely in skin tone, would—as testified—come to understand deeply, at a very early age, the profound path her life would take.

Testimony is a basic affirmation of something that is shared in human community. Well, the concerned neighbors who eventually gathered around Samuel and Patsy McLeod were living witnesses to a birth, their fifteenth child, regarded as entirely different. Albeit, Mary McLeod Bethune, as we have come to know her, was actually born in Mayesville, South Carolina, July 10, 1875, to the proud parents Sam and Patsy McLeod, hard-working and God-fearing people. It is reported by some biographers that her mother was a true matriarch with a gift for organization, while her father was a frugal and skillful farmer striving to improve his farm. But from the early rocking of the cradle, this newborn was perceived to be a different sort of child based on perceived testimony from neighborhood women:

> Neighbor women who were gathered there had in their minds the word "homely." Because of their shaking heads, the mother held her baby more closely and, out of her faith, stoutly replied, "*She is a child of prayer, Samuel.* I asked the Master to send us a child who would show us the way out. Of course, I expected He would bless us with a boy. But His will be done."

> The grandmother, Sophia, was rocking back and forth, puffing at her corncob pipe. She was murmuring, "Thank you, Master, for another grandchild. This is a different one. Thank you Master."[2]

It is only a glimpse into the obvious to suggest that the hearing of "testimonies" is not a ritual limited to courtroom law, but a recurring practice in the drama of black history and black religious experience in America. On her maternal side, the branches of the family tree (though the tribal origins are not exactly known) appear to run deep in the moral traditions and culture from Africa. For example, by way of family heritage, the mother of Mary Jane, Patsy McLeod, was apparently a descendent of a ruling family in Africa. At least, this is the claim, historically, of Rackham Holt, in his book, *Mary McLeod Bethune: A Biography.* As an interpreter of Bethune's moral thought, Holt aptly characterizes her material background in the following passage:

> Mary Jane's mother, now Patsy McLeod, was a delicate woman, small but regal in her bearing; she had the air of a princess. This she came by rightfully because, according to the family tradition, she was a descendant of a ruling family in Africa. Her matriarchal stateliness was apparent in her every movement. She was not able to read or write, but she had a precision of speech and a starched dignity, which forbade encroachments. Her feet and hands were beautiful, and these attributes were inherited by the daughter who was "different."[3]

In terms of social background, Mary Jane's father, Samuel McLeod, grew up on the old McLeod plantation, in the neighborhood of Mayesville. After taking Patsy's hand in marriage, which took place before Emancipation, Samuel McLeod displayed attributes from the care of his personality that indicated a man of moral strength and uncommon character. Rightly or wrongly perceived, many in the community of Mayesville regarded Samuel McLeod to be "black by nature, but proud by choice." Holt says, "He was a sturdy, medium-built colored man with clear features, a good farmer, with trained hands, a skillful carpenter and could work with tin ware and leather." Signifying an appreciative self-understanding, this good-natured African American male was a loving father, and succeeded along with his wife, Patsy, in establishing a healthy family foundation for Mary Jane in one's vision of the moral life. In tracing the development of Mary Jane's formative years, one can see the strong role of the family and the symbiotic relationship she had with her own mother and father. It is clear that while her mother had an unusual ability to organize and manage the essentials of family life, both parents contributed to the security and emotional well being of young Mary Jane McLeod.

Just as "testifying" involves the voice of the moral agent to speak: "In very truth I tell you, we speak of what we know, and we testify to what we have seen . . . " (John 3:11 NEB). So then, testimony keeps alive the reality of that which has happened. By the same token, the concept of "choosing" denotes a pattern of *authority-within* that "wills" one value over another. While the daughter of Sam and Patsy McLeod was seen as different, young Mary chose to light the *candle of prayer* as she remembered countless stories of the bullwhip days of slavery from the lips of her older brothers and sisters. To choose involves a deliberate act on the part of a person. It is a decision made, little or big. Therefore, to embrace the candle of prayer in search of the truth of one's past was a bold step by young Mary Jane to explore the moral contradictions and racial antipathies of her own social world.

Furthermore, the candle of prayer in the mind and heart of young Mary Jane was tantamount to power. There is a moral tradition in the black church that says: "Prayer changes things!" For example, throughout the bullwhip days of slavery, Mary Jane had heard her parents talk about how they had to secretly hide away to pray and to tell God all about their heartaches and troubles. As former slaves, Samuel and Patsy McLeod knew first hand the power of prayer, as it was integral to their social world of survival. Living on the ragged edges of racial bigotry, prayer for Mary Jane was not a *ritual* but a way of life. She always remembered her mother and grandmother Sophia literally talking to God while working and knitting from an old rocker on the porch, as if God were "a person actually present." Thus the inclination toward prayer as a source of power was not a religious ritual limited to Sunday morning worship, but a family discipline that was daily practiced morning, noon, and night in gratitude to God as the Creator and Sustainer of life. In the farming community of Mayesville, the power of prayer for young Mary Jane made a difference between acquiring the rudiments of learning and non-learning. In the tradition of the black church, Mary Jane would undoubtedly pray fervently loud: "Please, God have *somebody* teach me to read and write!"[4]

As a developing child, perhaps there is no act more brave or humbling as to stand up among family, friends, and neighbors to lay bare one's soul before God in the sanctuary of prayer. Yes, there is some truth in the saying, "prayer changes things!" Indeed, young Mary Jane had been taught to recognize, biblically and ethically, the power of prayer. To be sure, the candle of prayer means power. As Holy Scripture affirms: "A good person's prayer is powerful and effective" (Jas 5:16 NEB). The candle of prayer means knowledge. As Holy Scripture proclaims: "My people are destroyed for lack of knowledge" (Hos 4:6). By standing on the promises of God, this little girl from the rural community of Mayesville, who worked and picked cotton in brogan shoes, found a source of strength in the reality of prayer that would ultimately lay the foundation for higher learning and education. With working hands in the cotton field and a critical mind in the classroom, the candle of prayer not only beamed upon her the literary rays of light; but she taught a despised and rejected people how to fight. Put succinctly, young Mary Jane would later teach countless generations of African Americans how to use the basic rudiments of reading and writing as instruments to fight racial injustice in America.

Echoes of Personality and Power

Existentially, it has been said and some believe, that personality is the key to reality. The social norms and values presumed to be explicit in the Bible and reflected in the black church tradition have been considered to be *clues* in unpacking human personality. However, some people say that "power and personality" are like oil and water, they don't go together. But the ethically sensitive person must be suspicious of this claim. In Black–White relations of the Old South—especially in the Mayesville community of Mary Jane's childhood—who sets the standards for power? What is power in relation to personality? Certainly we may muse over the fact that Mary Jane's mother, Patsy McLeod, was a woman of small physical stature, but regal in *personality* and family tradition. In her own generation, personality is the moral equivalent of dignity. This was a way of affirming that people from diverse religious and cultural traditions—Red, Yellow, Black, and White—may not necessarily love you but, they must give you respect as a human being. Here personality is not the playhouse of power, but the gateway of true freedom for the oppressed.

Christians living in a secular culture seem to get confused about this word "power." For example, one religiously devout officer of the black church community once lamented to another:

> Deacon Jones, I ain't never wanted power . . . power corrupts good morals and one's prayer life in our church house . . . down here on earth. You can have all the world, just give me Jesus!

Well, it is only a glimpse into the obvious to suggest that Deacon Jones's friend had a rather confused notion of the interplay of power and personality. The famed theologian Reinhold Niebuhr would often define power as "the capacity to accomplish purpose." If we were to apply this standard of moral logic to the personality of young Mary Jane, it is reasonable to assume that Almighty God touched her life with a noble purpose.

For Mary Jane, it is apparent that power rooted in prayer accomplishes purpose. Like the candle of prayer, real power cannot only illuminate your path through the *thorns and thistles* of racial prejudice in society; but it can change you and re-arrange you as a child of God. It is no accident, therefore, that the first book that deeply influenced the worldview of young Mary Jane was the Bible. The moral traditions that she inherited from the household of Sam and Patsy McLeod placed a heavy emphasis on the Bible and the importance of individual initiative in the shaping of family life. In a sense, the dialectic of personality and power go hand-in-hand.

Positively considered, the boundary lines for understanding power in the emerging personality of young Mary Jane were not "control and greed," but "courage and grace." Here power is a by-product of the beauty of her own personality. A sense of human accountability to God and family, compassionately carried in behalf of friend or foe, best epitomizes the creative tensions between power and personality. Moral questions about longstanding suffering that still germinate in the popular thinking of African American culture and religion seem to read: Is God omnipotent or all-powerful? Is God all-loving and just? If God is all-powerful and all-loving, why did a loving God allow an unloving system of chattel slavery to be fastened on the backs of Africans for over 350 years?

More specifically one must ask, What is the relation between human greed and God's grace as reflected in the life and times of Mary McLeod Bethune? What is the meaning of God's grace for a people deeply acquainted with oppression and the *songs of sorrow* in American society? For Mary McLeod Bethune, what is the link between education and self-determination on the part of America's youth? What sort of moral teachings are necessary in our global community to create and sustain a just social order?

In this regard, our ethical inquiry into the life, religious beliefs, and times of Mary McLeod Bethune will not only illuminate all of these pivotal questions and issues; but it cracks open a window of understanding—where in her own narrative light (i.e., her "personality") may become our beacon (i.e., our "power"). Concerning the spiritual source of power, Mohandas K. Gandhi once remarked: "There is a soul force in the universe, which, if we permit it, will flow through us and produce."

The Birth of a Dream: Education

Mary McLeod Bethune, a visionary with a morally resilient personality, had a dream of providing education for economically impoverished young black girls in the Deep South. Like the story of the young Joseph in Egypt who helped to save his own family from the claws of famine and oppression, Mary McLeod Bethune had a dream that would, inevitably, impact the changing patterns of education for blacks in America. There were none quite like this "peculiar child" who hailed from Mayesville, South Carolina—one who viewed education not only essential for black survival in a hostile white world; but education *per se*, was understood as a stepping-stone to success.

Mary McLeod Bethune was truly one of the pioneer educators of the twentieth century. As the fifteenth of seventeen children, hailing from the tiny hamlet of Mayesville, she did not seek this extraordinary designation of "pioneer educator" but the peculiar fragments of history made it so. From the early rocking of her cradle it is apparent that Mary Jane pleaded and cried out to God about the dream of education and deliverance:

> Dear God . . . help me to get educated. Please, help me to read the Bible. O Lord, deliver me from the crab grass.[5]

In taking inventory of one's own spiritual pilgrimage, the social critic may be inclined to say that "history is always partial to irony and surprise." At the time this prayer was apparently uttered, Mary Jane was only nine years old, working hard picking cotton at the McLeod plantation—a customary practice of survival on the part of ex-slaves and common laborers. Perhaps the social critic would logically ask: Does God really care about a nine-year-old girl with a dream of education from the cotton fields of Mayesville? Does God bother to answer the prayers of children? What sort of "crab grass" must our children seek deliverance from in today's society?

Well, for young Mary Jane, she discovered something about the loving nature of God, who is Deliverer. For example, the psalmist declares: "I sought the Lord, and he answered me, and delivered me from all my fears. Look to him, and be radiant; so your faces shall never be ashamed" (Ps 34:4–5 NRSV). Prayer is a response, a burning cry to God, regarding the critical conditions of life. Genuine prayer is often frustrated by our own sense of self-importance or self-pity in the community of faith. But young Mary Jane was apparently tempted by neither vanity nor pity. We may say that the word "pity" means to be perpetually quarrelsome by taking on the so-called *poor-little-me* syndrome. It would seem that young Mary Jane never saw herself as a "poor-little-me," but a loving child of God—capable of learning and leading others toward the dream of education.

Concretely speaking, the birth of a dream in the life of Mary Jane found expression as one Miss Wilson, a Negro missionary from the board of the Presbyterian Church, stopped by the McLeod plantation. It was here in the community of Mayesville—as she was selected by her parents to attend a newly formed school—where a vision by Mary Jane was beginning to take shape that would, inevitably, impact her life work. Accordingly, one day in school Miss Wilson presented Mary Jane with a Bible. Of course, the Bible is often referred to in the black religious community as the "Good Book." It was then and is now regarded by many Christians not only as the "living Word of God," a "repository of divine wisdom, love, and salvation" in order to make it to heaven; but it is also understood by many African American Christians as a source of moral guidance, education, and prosperity on earth. Therefore, the whole notion of the Bible as the Good Book, at the practical level, meant that slaves and ex-slaves had something to hold on to as a tool of survival in a hostile white world. In a post-slavery society during the Reconstruction Era in which Mary Jane was born, the Bible was the first book blacks learned to read. The thirst for education or religious instruction among ex-slaves were so great until they would literally sneak lessons whenever a teacher could be found.[6]

This is why the Bible was referred to in the parlance of black-folk culture as essentially "the Good Book." Ethically considered, this meant that for Mary Jane and many of her contemporaries the Bible was not necessarily understood as some heavenly roadmap descriptive of a *pie-in-the-sky* theology after the human person leaves this world; rather the Bible—to paraphrase the renowned educator Benjamin E. Mays, former President of Morehouse College, Atlanta, Georgia—was viewed by blacks as a nursery of learning. Be that as it may, Mary Jane was schooled in the reading of the Bible and fascinated by the deep things of God. Apparently, one of her favorite Scriptures was John 3:16 which reads:

> For God so loved the world, that he gave his only begotten Son, that whosoever believeth in Him should not perish but have everlasting life.

It has been said and some biographers believe, that no doubt a "little light" revelation went off in Mary Jane's head around the risky pronoun "whosoever." In this contemporary age of consumption and secularism where it is more important to be politically correct than racially inclusive, it struck Mary Jane that the "whosoever" in this popular biblical text referred to "her" and "all people," regardless of race, religion, class, creed, or color. Put another way, the dream of education is not limited by skin color or gender orientation. Accordingly, Mary Jane, being persistent in her prayer life, was awarded a scholarship to attend Scotia Seminary in Concord, North Carolina, as a result of assistance by a Quaker woman named Mary Crissman. It was here at Scotia that much of the social, religious, and moral teachings of the Christian faith began to shape and nurture the character and lifework of Mary Jane McLeod.

With the emerging dream of becoming a missionary to Africa, she was later awarded another scholarship to attend Moody Bible Institute in Chicago. Upon graduation from Moody Institute, her heart was set on going to Africa as a missionary; however, the gods of disappointment slammed the door on that opportunity and Mary Jane McLeod then made a turn toward Augusta, Georgia, where she served as a teacher at Haines Institute.

At the age of 24, in the prime of young adulthood while accepting another teaching post at a mission school in Sumter, South Carolina, Mary Jane's life was ripe for a dramatic change. Here she met a rather shy teacher named Albertus Bethune. While Mary Jane's educational aspirations knew no limits, the emerging friendship mushroomed into a serious romance and they were happily married in 1898. To this marital union was born her only son, Albert, in the southern genteel city of Savannah, Georgia, where Mr. Bethune opened up a tailor shop.[7]

Perhaps it is not incidental to note that the black church, as a social institution, has always been a cultural center for the enhancement of positive moral and spiritual values between men and women. So then, it is only a romantic glimpse into the obvious to suggest the "church house" was the initial meeting place for Mary Jane and Albertus Bethune. In Rackham Holt's classic book *Mary McLeod Bethune: A Biography*, the author observed this pivotal social encounter in the following manner:

> Mary, always a participant in whatever was going on about her . . . had joined the church choir as a matter of course. There she met a young man, "tall, dark, and handsome," with a most appealing tenor voice which blended very nicely with hers. Albertus Bethune was an intelligent . . . sensitive man who . . . then working in the men's clothing section of a department store . . . for the past three years Mary had not put much thought upon young men. Her earlier flirtatiousness had been totally submerged in an absorption with her work and what . . . she intended to make of herself.[8]

Mary, still young in life, was a deeply religious and moral person, one given to discipline in the puritan values of hard work, frugality, and loving nurture in matters of home and family life. It was six months after Samuel and Patsy McLeod had experienced the satisfaction of their nineteenth grandchild that Mary received an offer from Rev. C. J. Uggans, pastor of the Presbyterian Church in Palatka, Florida, to move there and establish a new school. It goes without saying that Rev. Uggans was already familiar with Mary's impressive record of educational achievement. Therefore, the idea of undertaking the new school symbolized a profound opportunity to incorporate in America's Southland the purposive essence of her missionary training: the development of a school for girls and young people.

From City Dump to School Discipline

In the struggle to unmask a vision that would save young southern children from the sin of aimlessness, Mary McLeod Bethune had the courage to build a school. Under the high waving flags of "Dixie culture" and the southern confederacy, this vision on the part of Dr. Bethune was not necessarily to save young people of her own day from the current scars of drugs, gang violence, teen pregnancy or welfare dependency; rather, it was a dream born of the hope to make human life more human for children and adults at Daytona Beach, Florida who were victimized by the demons of poverty and racial bigotry.

In the thoughtful volume *The College Built on Prayer: Mary McLeod Bethune*, Jesse Walter Dees offers the reader a portrait of the economic and social conditions that ordinary Negro laborers faced as Dr. Bethune arrived at Daytona Beach in September 1904. He wrote:

> Mrs. Bethune had heard that there was a great need at Daytona Beach, where many Negroes were said to live in poverty . . . and squalid conditions. God seemed to direct her to Daytona Beach.

It was too late to return when her Palatka house burned down, and later her husband died. Arriving in Daytona Beach with only her personal belongings and her five-year old son, Albert, Mrs. Bethune found living conditions worse than she had expected. And she found . . . that the Negro population was indifferent to her dream of a new school.[9]

Notwithstanding, the dream of a new school was not to be denied for this extraordinary woman of courage. It was in the same year of our Lord, 1904, that Dr. Bethune found—by the grace of God—an old empty shack on Oak Street in Daytona Beach, located a few blocks away from the railroad tracks and city dump. Here she skillfully negotiated with the owner to rent the empty shack for $11 a month.[10] Perhaps in the heart and mind of Dr. Bethune, she carefully pondered the ethical questions: Will this humble beginning become a miracle or a mess? Will the Negro population of Daytona Beach move from indifference to acceptance of my dream for a new school? How can one's vision of a school and the basic disciplines of survival for Negro children become a reality? Can anything good come from a city dump? What would be the cost, educationally, of a dream deferred? What if I—though honestly seeking to establish a new school—fail? As people of faith and conscience, it was hard to imagine or "second-guess" in our time the sort of difficult questions that must have run through the mind of Dr. Bethune in 1904.

Although this empty shack on Oak Street was rented out to Dr. Bethune for $11.00 per month, she could only offer $1.50, and the gracious owner trusted her to pay the rest as she sold sweet potato pies, performed old Negro spirituals for sympathetic whites, and learned how, above all, to literally lean on *the everlasting arms of Jesus*! As an extraordinary woman of courage, Dr. Bethune founded the school on October 3, 1904, which originally bore the name of the Daytona Educational and Industrial Training School for Negro Girls.[11] According to the biographer Jesse Walter Dees, Jr., former professor of Social Science at Bethune-Cookman College, the first students that gave birth to this school consisted of "five little girls whose parents agreed to pay $.50 a week tuition, and her (Mrs. Bethune's) five-year-old son, Albert."[12] In probing closely into the life and morals of this extraordinary woman of courage, one is struck by her holistic vision of education inclusive of the religious, cultural, and industrial dimensions of human life itself. For example, Professor Dees reminds us that for Dr. Bethune, the very first day of school—nurtured in the loving tradition of the black church experience—began with the hymn: "*Leaning on the Everlasting Arms*" and "The 23rd Psalm." Reflecting in part, the industrial philosophy of self-reliance, explicit in the thought of Booker T. Washington of this social era, Dr. Bethune's vision of education was radically pragmatic for young black youths of the Daytona Beach community. Concerning the school's curriculum and its pragmatic outlook, Dees makes the following observations:

> The curriculum at the first school placed great emphasis on domestic and industrial training. The girls learned crafts and homemaking. The students were taught to cook and sew along with reading, writing, and arithmetic.[13]

In the course of the school's rich history and religio-cultural development, Dr. Bethune as teacher and principal not only nurtured the five little girls and her son Albert in the disciplines of industrial education, but she also taught them about the unitive spirit of *grace* within. She taught them something about a God of love who wants to utilize the students' total lives (i.e., head, heart, hands, soul, and spirit) for a wider vision of education and human fulfillment. She taught these little girls and her own son the disciplines of self-giving love and public service. As school principal and a woman of courage, Dr. Bethune taught them the meaning of *grace* under the groaning and striving to make life better for young Negro children who lived on the wrong side of the tracks in the Daytona black community. She gave this first generation of graduates not only vision but *voice*. Indeed, their persistent strivings and hard work helped to form a marvelous choir, The Bethune Choral Group—as they were affectionately called—that sang "spirituals and hymns in some of the finest homes, churches, and hotels in fashionable Daytona Beach."[14] In short, the genius of Mary McLeod Bethune as a pioneer educator and woman of courage was that she gave these five little girls, and her own son positive self-esteem and a passion to serve the downtrodden and the hurting ones among us. It is only a glimpse into the obvious to suggest that Dr. Bethune gave these five little girls not only roots but wings. It was a way of affirming, in the religio-cultural milieu of the black church family, the cryptic wisdom: "it is not where you come from that counts, but where you're going that matters!" Hence, their reality was such that they literally moved "from city dump to school discipline." Their light, therefore, is still our beacon today.

Passion for Learning

In contemporary society there are many of us *dripping* with a passion for learning, yet there are too many more who have given up on our children and their potential for success. Some social critics in contemporary society may even be tempted to label our children as members of the "Lost Generation" or what sociologists called "Generation X"—a generation without clear direction or one preoccupied with an ethic of "me-ism." Well, it is obvious from historical records that Mary McLeod Bethune was never in a fan club for quitters and losers. Indeed, the truth of the matter is that no such terminology, comparatively speaking, as "Generation X" had even been created by social scientists of her own day. Her passion for learning was apparently not driven by the social forces of individualism and crass materialism so pervasive in our contemporary *me-centered* culture. Rather the desire to learn as a mature adult was as deep as the Atlantic Ocean on whose shores she would often walk and meditate along the seamless skyline of Daytona Beach. For example, it seems to me that her vision reflected what Brian Wren calls "education for justice," the conscious act of changing the conditions in which we live.[15]

I am reminded of a famous proverb from eastern Africa concerning the value of education which reads: "Education is an ocean and every child must have the right to set sail!" The echoing philosophy of education implicit in the moral teachings of Dr. Bethune was the view that each child in America must have equal opportunity to develop his or her potentiality regardless of race, religion, or gender orientation. Each child is entitled to learning and must be given, educationally, "the right to set sail" upon the ocean of life.

Moreover, we have already suggested that Dr. Bethune's passion for learning involved not only the creation of a school (e.g., domestic and industrial training) where girls were crafted in the art of homemaking along with reading, writing and arithmetic; but there was also an emphasis on the creation of an ethos in which genuine freedom, creativity, and individuality were allowed to flourish amid the nefarious realities of racial injustice, demoralization, and *de jure* segregation around the turn of the twentieth century. Within two years of its inception on October 3, 1904, Dr. Bethune's passion for learning and her prudent efforts of hard work led to an increase of students from 5 to 250 pupils, with 4 teachers.

However, we may say that the initial success in student enrollment came with a price. By this, I mean to suggest that the new difficulty faced by Dr. Bethune was the choice of increasing the cost of feeding the students and paying the rent, on the one hand; or the decision to build her own schoolhouse, on the other. She chose the latter. Apparently, the only available land for her own schoolhouse was the city dump, known as "Hell's Hole." Perhaps it would be noteworthy to the reader to observe Professor Dees's graphic description of the location for the schoolhouse:

> . . . "Hell's Hole," full of tin cans, bottles, garbage, frogs, and thousands of mosquitoes. The owner agreed to sell the land for $200.00 with $5.00 down and the balance to be paid in two years. Mrs. Bethune returned a few days later . . . with her down payment. And in order to raise further funds for her school, she spoke or sang with her group all over the community, begged money, rang doorbells . . . riding around town on her little bicycle.[16]

Reflecting on Dr. Bethune's passion for learning and the desire to establish a school, we are challenged to remember, in the ironic words of Charles Dickens, "we live in the best of times and the worst of times." To be sure, Dr. Bethune had to walk, beg, sing, and sell sweet potato pies in order to keep the dream of education alive for young black children. Her moral will was stubborn as polished steel; and her passion for learning was unrelenting as the beaming sun that loomed over Daytona Beach—especially for the sons and daughters of ex-slaves. In short, we may say that consistently and persistently Dr. Bethune's passion for learning can be seen in a key moral dictum that she passed on from one generation of students to another: "Be an artist in all you do."[17] From a heart and mind vibrant with a passion for education, Dr. Bethune encouraged her students to resist the pitfalls of despair and racial degradation so much a part of growing up black in the southern culture. Instead, she readily advocated the values of equal opportunity, self-discipline, and faith as indispensable in human life. Poetically, the metaphor of the strong black woman as leader and educator captures the spirit of what it means to be fully human. For example, the African writer Benson Ebinne, in his poem "*Ode to the Southern Woman*," puts the matter this way:

> All her life
> She'd seen many
> Thirsty, tongue-parched
> People sing the blues:
> Tunes of hope,
> Vibrations through souls,
> Souls bereft of the waters
> Of equal opportunity.

All her life
She'd traveled the wilderness
With her eyes trained on the pool.
Now, old and wiser
And armed only with a stick
And the courage of the hoary headed,
She takes the steps
Of the thousand mile journey,
Runs the gauntlet,
Grasps the fountain spout,
Douses her thirsty throat,
And dares the gauntlet
To stir.[18]

God of a Second Chance

Our glimpse into the life and moral teachings of Mary McLeod Bethune validates the importance of education and critical learning in the character formation of young people. As a Christian leader and visionary, she took seriously the educational imperative implicit in the Gospel of Matthew: "Take my yoke upon you, and learn of me" (Matt 11:29 KJV). Indeed, the challenge to learn and grow was at the heart of her passion to build a new school for the rejected and despised youths of the wider Daytona Beach community. They were often regarded by the dominant white culture as "inferior" and "second-class citizens" and not worthy of formal education and training. Now the genius of Dr. Bethune's philosophy and moral passion was to take these largely poor and culturally despised youths and literally give them *a second chance.*

The notion of a second chance means many things to different people. For Sam and Patsy McLeod, the very idea of a second chance meant the sudden recognition that their fifteenth child was something unique from the beginning. One can only imagine the profound excitement that must have echoed in the voice of Grandma Sophia at Mary Jane's birth: "Someone go get Sam from the cotton fields," she might have said, "He's got to come in right now and see this new baby . . . she's something special!" It is said, and some believe, that Sam McLeod, for example, left his tools or cotton sack in the field in the middle of the day to come and see this gift from God, a new baby destined for greatness. Each human life is a gift of God. Each new life is a gift of grace. "Who we are" is a by-product of family heritage and social history. But *"Whose we are"* is *only by grace.*

Now, the upshot of what I am trying to suggest here is that ultimately it is grace divine that gives us a second chance.

In the early life and development of Mary McLeod Bethune, we may observe another illustration of what it means to have a second chance. In the love-filled home of the McLeod family, after the daily chores were done, Mary would often take the family Bible from its special shelf. "Some day I will read this . . . please God, let me learn to read. If there's a way, show it to me!"[19] Now at the time, Mary was eleven years old and still couldn't read, not because she was a "slow learner," but because of a southern segregationist tradition of racial bigotry which denied black children the opportunity to read or write. As the story unfolds, the whole McLeod family was attentively working in the fields when suddenly there came walking down the road a stranger who called out:

> "Hello!" I am Miss Wilson. My church wants me to open a school nearby. I'm looking for students . . . Can you send me any of your children to my school?"[20]

The upshot of this true narrative is that the prayers and hopes of the McLeod family were answered. In summary, it seems to me that one of the critical lessons to be gleaned from the early life of Mary McLeod is the fact that she not only learned to read and do basic arithmetic, but went on to provide *a second chance* for five little girls and her son on a special autumn day (October 3, 1904) in the Daytona Beach community. Secondly, it is important to remember that the birth of a dream in the form of establishing the Daytona Educational and Industrial Training School for Negro Girls, as it was initially called, involved a lifelong commitment to learning. The very idea of education or learning seems to suggest to us in contemporary society a new openness to learning on the part of us all. Thirdly, we need today as never before in our culture a certain passion in education, both public and private, which cries out to the world: "Give our children and troubled youths a second chance!"

Generally, education is defined as a process of critical learning and being deeply concerned with the development of each child or individual from one stage of growth to another. We are reminded that for Mary McLeod Bethune, education involved the unitive threads of head, heart, and hands working in concert for the common good. Education *per se*, is not static but dynamic. Education, in the critical thought of Mary McLeod Bethune, is more than learned behavior based on prescribed materials in a given curriculum. Rather it is a process designed to "draw out" or "draw forth." In short, Dr. Bethune strongly believed that education involved giving each child, though poor or rich in society, a second chance.

We have already suggested that one of the recurring moral values present throughout Dr. Bethune's extraordinary life is the passion for learning. As a child she would walk five miles back and forth each day in order to drink from the fountain of learning. As soon as she would acquire new knowledge in human community, other people, both young and old, would benefit. However, we would be quick to add that her philosophy of learning was radically inclusive of both the personal and social, as well as the religious and ethical dimension of human existence. With a kind of moral zeal equivalent to a devout missionary, Mary McLeod Bethune's early testimony is as striking as it is revealing. Jesse Walter Dees, in his book *The College Built on Prayer*, puts the matter this way regarding her formative years:

> At that time there were no schools for Negroes less than three hundred miles away, and Mary Jane trudged back and forth the narrow dirt road to the one-room school where she learned to read and use numbers.[21]

Like refreshing water from a babbling brook, like a grace-filled revelation from heaven, Dr. Bethune imagined a world of learning and spiritual formation. For example, there is the story of her being given a Bible by her beloved teacher, and she often read from the Bible St. Paul's advice to Timothy in the majestic words: "Study to show thyself approved unto God, a worker who has no need to be ashamed, rightly explaining the word of truth" (2 Tim 2:15). This text gripped her soul, as one nurtured in humble beginnings from South Carolina. Apparently this powerful self-revelation ignited in Dr. Bethune vistas of understanding that anybody can become somebody, when a person's life is placed in the hands of God. There is within the word "study" a universal echo that seems to transcend all barriers of gender, race, class or religion. So then, the seed of learning grew out of Dr. Bethune's awareness that God really does care about the education and well-being of all people—in their struggle to attain a fuller life.

Another important moral teaching peculiar to Dr. Bethune's philosophy of education was the value placed on "dignified labor." Historically considered, we may say that in her day and time, the social philosophy that she shared was shaped, in part, by the enormous influence and national repetition of Booker T. Washington. They both were guardians of a vision: the vision of economic self-reliance.

Guardians of the Vision

As the drama of black life unfolded on the American scene during the first three decades of the twentieth century, Booker T. Washington and Mary McLeod Bethune emerged as prominent black leaders in support of a concept of education as "self-reliance" and the importance of dignified labor. For example, in the classic book *The Story of My Life and Work*, Booker T. Washington highlights the philosophy of self-reliance and self-help when he states, "No race can prosper till it learns that there is as much dignity in tilling a field as in writing a poem.[22] As a guardian of the vision, Mary McLeod Bethune followed the example of Booker T. Washington by advocating the concerns for economic self-reliance, dignified labor, integrity in business practices, and faithfulness in the religious life. Comparatively speaking, both visionary leaders believed that the self-reliant person is one who knows that "it takes as much skill in using one's hands as one's brain" in service of the common good. For example, in his book *Liberating Vision*, Robert Franklin makes a cogently relevant observation about Washington's pragmatic philosophy of dignified labor. He writes:

> In an effort to dignify common labor, he had to disassociate the labor of free men and women and its virtues from the familiar forced, dehumanizing labor of the slave era. In 1907, he delivered two speeches on the economic development of the Negro race in slavery and since emancipation . . . While drawing sharp contrast between slave and free labor, he began to advance his case for the ennobling effects of the Puritan work ethic.[23]

Here it is the intent of the writer to demonstrate how both Washington and Bethune were essentially guardians of the same vision for an oppressed and dehumanized generation of black youth. They advocated a philosophy of self-reliance, which included a concern for the total well being of each person: economically, spiritually, physically, and morally. "Thus, the authentic person," says Franklin, "would be a laborer who possessed distinctive and refined agricultural or industrial skill and who could provide desired services in the local community." Accordingly, Dr. Bethune underscored the value of dignified labor in the totality of human development by making the following observations in her Founder's Day address on October 3, 1936. For Bethune, the winds of human progress always involve mind, body, and spirit—i.e., faith in the promises of God.

Expressing gratitude, faith, and pride in this historic institution, she proclaimed:

> Here is a plant, conservatively speaking, a million dollars, started in Faith, boys and girls, thirty-two years ago with a dollar and a half payment, a desire to serve, Faith in God, and in one's self. Take this institution you have, believe in God, believe in yourself, and step out and do something! It takes time to be done. This has been done, and I am going to expect you as the years go by to do greater things, for your opportunities are far greater than mine have ever been. God bless you, young people. This is for you. Dig deeper, apply yourself, be diligent, learn to work beautifully with your hands—"Dignify Labor."[24]

Given the pragmatic philosophy of Dr. Bethune, working class people not only embraced an ethic of self-reliance, but they began to see the virtue of dignified labor. Economic self-reliance requires the daily use of both head and hands. In her own social era, she declared that blacks must become producers not simply consumers. Here Bethune further stated:

> We need more men, more women in the world who are willing to work with their hands. We need more producers, we need more boys and girls to take your science and go out and develop that cultured field. . . . Learn to be more useful. . . . Go out and do! The world is calling for men and women who can do things—not only with their brains, but behind their brains they need trained hands to meet the great issues of today. May we depend upon the students of Bethune-Cookman College, that the ideas and ideals thrown out by the teachers and workers of this institution, add to that great need—galleries of producers. Men and women who are not afraid and ashamed to work.[25]

Faith and Frugality

In a moral and religious sense, the virtues of faith and frugality were perceived as complimentary parts of a viable value system for black progress. As an exceedingly perceptive leader, Dr. Bethune had internalized some of the prevailing social values of her own day, as expressed in Booker T. Washington's famous moral dictum: "Cast down your buckets where you are." Indeed, we may rightly affirm that Washington's social philosophy was the dominant moral framework for black progress in America's post-Industrial Revolution, where people were encouraged to cultivate the civic virtues of hard work, individualism, thrift, investment, and frugality.

Normatively, it is only a glimpse into the obvious to suggest that the moral and religious landscape that shaped Dr. Bethune's worldview involved the language of *faith* and *frugality*. Perhaps the biblical passage in her thought that best illuminates this creative tension between faith and frugality is Philippians 2:12: "work out your own salvation with fear and trembling." Holy Scripture further affirms in the heart and mind of the believer: "for it is God which worketh in you both to will and to do of his good pleasure" (Phil 2:13). It would seem to me that Bethune's understanding of the language of faith and frugality served to inspire a generation of young people to believe that there is as much dignity in plowing the cotton fields as writing a poem; there is as much dignity in the work of a janitor's broom as an artist's paint brush; and there is as much dignity in the seamstress's hands of designing clothes as in the architect's hands of designing modern buildings. For Dr. Bethune, the normative bottom line is that we are all under the divine imperative to "work out our own Salvation" (Phil 2:12), and to embrace certain living habits that inspire us to be the best we can be—regardless of our social position or economic stratum in society.

For example, when the morally sensitive person takes a closer look at this word "frugality," we may discern that it means "thriftiness," "not wasteful," "useful," "temperate." Etymologically speaking, it is derived from the Latin *frugalis*, which means, "fit for food." Now in a moral and religious sense, there is another kind of "food" that pressed in upon Mary Bethune's consciousness, namely, the "spiritual food" of faith. Such a "food" in the religious thinking of Mary Bethune endows each struggling believer with purpose and guidance. In short, I contend that the flipside of frugality is faith, as reflected in the critical thought of Mary Bethune, because each has to do with purposive living as guided by God. Accordingly, the biographer Audrey Thomas McCluskey wrote:

> Bethune proclaimed a personal relationship with God that emanated from her devout family and rural Christian community. She liked to stress that she was on a mission dictated by God, and that her faith and her work justified each other.[26]

Faith and Social Progress

In America's society where blacks and other minorities have been victimized by social bigotry and injustice, Mary Bethune advocated a *notion* of faith tied in with social progress in human community. In the perceptive volume *Mary McLeod Bethune in Religious Perspective*, the author Clarence

Newsome carefully points out that one of the most interesting aspects of Mary Bethune's career was not the reality of her deep religious faith, which she possessed, but how that faith impacted one's interpretation of the mission of the church. For example, as a woman who attended Moody Bible Institute, Mary Bethune had prepared herself to do missionary work in Africa with a Presbyterian mission board; but after graduating in the 1890s she was, unfortunately, told that "there are no openings for black missionaries in Africa." For whatever reasons, she was ethically burdened by the "double handicap" of being a black woman and a trained missionary.

In any event, Mary Bethune understood herself to be a missionary in a morally progressive way. Theologically, she identified the missionary role of the church with the question of social reform or progress beyond its institutional structure. What I am trying to suggest here is that Mary Bethune did not operate entirely outside of the church's traditional structures; rather, she interpreted those structures with a broader educational vision in view. Newsome states that, "by identifying with the role she was able to determine the nature of and exercise control over activity which, in her mind at least, legitimately extended the work of the church."[27] To be candid about the matter of a broader vision, we may rightly say that Mary Bethune "looked upon the church as an institution whose most important concern is the welfare of persons."[28] Therefore, I suspect that implicit in her *notion of faith* is the recognition that the basic concept of faith itself must be relevant to the issue of "social progress" on the part of each individual as a child of God. Put another way, spiritual growth cannot be separated from social progress—since we know that faith calls us to do ministry for the common welfare of all persons in this world. Here Mary Bethune emphatically asserted:

> There are many false ideas about the spiritual glow which . . . is supposed to characterize the Negro soul. The truth is the Negro long lived on a revivalistic emotion and was taught to think of heaven as a land of luxury to which he would pass after a life of burden in this world. The Negro needs an equality of religion. (He needs a religion in which) his religious feeling has . . . matured into . . . social passion . . . [29]

For Mary Bethune true faith requires a religion that sees the church operating with a missionary vision of "social passion" for the welfare of all people. In a moral and religious sense, social progress is a by-product of social passion. Social progress in the ethical thought of Mary Bethune is a result of struggle and faith in a personal God who will not only see us through; but rather, a personal God who empowers us to *press onward* toward the mark despite the difficulties of human life. In short, reflecting on her long faith journey with God, Bethune remembers: "God gave me faith in myself and in my fellow man. This faith which has removed doubt and kept me pressing onward and upward in spite of difficulties brought one an *open mind*. Through this open mind, I have learned about God's people and God's world."[30]

The Search for a Viable Ethic

At the fundamental levels of black life we must raise the questions not only "what is ethics?" but what has ethics to do with the faith and educational legacy of Mary McLeod Bethune? For Christians and secular persons, what has ethics to do with the human struggle to improve the plight and educational opportunity of people of color in American society? From the outset, we may observe that the moral values and beliefs of Mary McLeod Bethune were deeply rooted in the black religious tradition. Ethics originates in everyday life. It would be a mistake to regard ethics as a purely "theoretical" or "academic" study having no intimate connections with the trials and tribulations of ordinary people seeking to survive and find happiness in human life. For Bethune, Jesus was the supreme paradigm for the moral life of faith and service in the wider society. She followed tenaciously the biblical text that echoed: "If anyone serves me, he (or she) must follow me; where I am, my servant will be. Whoever serves me will be honored by my Father" (John 12:26 NEB). For Dr. Bethune, it is especially noteworthy that gospel tradition is full of the practical teachings of Jesus (e.g., the Sermon on the Mount, Matt 6:1–34; the dual love commandment, Matt 22:36–40; and the parables of the sower and the mustard seed, Mark 4:1–41), and all of these sources of faith and enlightenment tell us something about what is required of us are on the Christian moral life. In either good times or hard times, Mary Bethune embraced the sort of moral value system which encouraged her students on the college campus to sing: "*Be not dismayed, whatever betide, God will take care of you!*" The moral strength and power of her words made a difference for friends and foes alike, because the "moral message and the messenger were the same."

When the rhetoric of ethical reflection clears in the public arena of education and moral struggle, what we find is a powerful woman of character whose faith is rooted in the gospel of Jesus Christ and in a peculiar God of love who sides with the working poor and those who believe in dignified labor. Because Mary Bethune knew, firsthand, the moral contradictions of racial bigotry and democracy, she embraced an understanding of ethics in the Christian moral life that could either make one *bitter* or *better*. She chose the latter. Concretely, what then, is at stake in fostering one's ethical understanding of education and faith?

The search for a viable ethic must necessarily start with the discipline of ethics itself. For the intellectually curious person, the word "ethics" is derived from the Greek *ethos* and the Latin term *mos*. The former refers to a stall or dwelling, whereas the latter means custom or usage as prescribed by the practices of a given community. Thus the term *ethos* refers to a web of values or beliefs that function to hold together our sense of community identity, and culture. Accordingly, we may say that our decisions about good and evil, appropriate and inappropriate behavior, about right and wrong are fundamentally *ethos* questions. By comparative logic, the same word "morality" is a derivative from the Latin term *mos*, which are set "mores." Therefore, a useful distinction here may be that ethics can be defined as behavior according to reasons, whereas morality is behavior according to custom. Like religion, morality is subject to the peculiar configurations of history and its cultural imprints. For example, in the structured patterns of black-white relationships during the early days of Dr. Bethune's childhood, a so-called "colored girl" was forbidden to go to public schools with a "white girl." Here we may observe that segregationist *customs* in the Old South denied blacks the opportunity for social integration or educational interaction. The conventional logic of the segregationist functioned in a customary way, to not only legitimate white control and cultural dominance, but to literally keep the black man in "his place." The prevailing attitudes of conventional morality went something like this in the twisted mindset of the segregationist in regard to the social status of blacks in American society:

If you're white, you are all right
If you're yellow, you are mellow
If you're brown, stick around;
But if you're black
Get back!

The strange and dazzling world of racial stereotypes in America does not conform to easy definitions of ethics and morality. Enthroned and shaped by layers of tradition and customary morality, the segregationist tends to see the world through eyeglasses of power and racial domination—where one can blindly affirm, "if you're white, you are all right." This perception of things based on status or skin color in the social order is less a product of ethics, and more a by-product of "southern customs" or shall we say, customary patterns of traditional morality. The upshot of the critical problem here is one of moral discernment. The naughty fact to be discerned in black-white relations is to see the thick wall built around "racist customs." The real challenge for people of goodwill demands constructing a *bridge* over racist American customs—in order that true democracy may breathe in our nation.

Comparatively speaking, it is not enough to understand that "morality means behavior according to custom;" rather we move beyond customary thinking to critical thinking, which literally calls in the question the customary attitude of the segregationist that "if you're white, you are all right . . . if you're brown, stick around, but if you're black, get back." Moreover, it is only a glimpse into the obvious to suggest that Mary Bethune went beyond the dangerous waters of customary morality—deeply ingrained in the parlance of Anglo-American culture and religion—in search of a viable ethic to guide her educational vision. Indeed, we may point out that in the corpus of her educational vision was the moral conviction that one person with God can make a difference. Therefore, a viable ethic must consist of both faith and work. As the Bible reminds us: "for as the body without the spirit is dead, so faith without works is dead also" (Jas 2:26).

For Mary Bethune, a viable ethic of faith tells us how the light of education can banish the darkness of ignorance. A viable ethic of faith tells us how the dreary paths of racial bigotry can be transformed and blossom. It tells us that someday life's wrongs, by God's grace, will be made right. "I feel my faith and my work haul justified each other,"[31] says Dr. Bethune. Furthermore, a viable ethic of faith enabled her to proclaim something about the spiritual and moral character of life itself. In her own words: "my life has been a spiritual thing, a religious reality, creative and alive."[32] Thus through a viable ethic of faith what was once a mere educational vision became a reality. Faith is a gift of God. Faith clothes one's fragile dreams with the explosive power of a mustard seed—where the wasteland of a city dump becomes the cornerstone of a school. In short, for Mary McLeod Bethune a viable ethic of faith always "demands what seems impossible." In 1954 in a speech entitled "*My Faith and My Job*," Dr. Bethune summarizes the whole matter of faith—in light of her vision of an institution—in this manner:

> Through the eye of faith I saw more than a city dumping pile when at last I found the place to plant the school I had so long envisaged. With my own hands I began to remove the refuse from the land in which I had at the beginning literally only pennies to invest. The

first building to grace what is now a lively campus was appropri-
ately called "Faith Hill," and it was dedicated to the mission out of
which it was conceived.[33]

Faith can make a difference. It is what the church of the living God is
built upon. In the course of human struggle as an ethicist, theologian, and
follower of Christ, I have discovered that very little can be accomplished
in life without faith and a vision for the common good. In short, the life
of Mary McLeod Bethune embodies the best of the black church tradition
with its emphasis on faith, freedom, justice, equality, fortitude, prudence,
and a passion for education. Her warning to Christians in contemporary
society is urgently sound as it is prophetic: unless we regain the true essence of the values and virtues of black church tradition, we are headed
for moral anarchy. We are headed—if we do not press back the tides of
hedonism and relativism—for spiritual bankruptcy in a society without a
sense of divine presence and moral boundaries. Yet Dr. Bethune fervently
admonished the generation of her own contemporaries, in familiar language of the biblical text, to "be strong in the grace that is in Christ Jesus;
and what you have heard," says Paul, "from me though many witnesses
entrust to faithful people who will be able to teach others as well" (2 Tim.
2:1–2). Undoubtedly, what is at stake here is the importance of faith in
every aspect of one's life. Faith is entrustment and reliance upon Christ
Jesus in good times as well as bad times, because God is faithful to us in
human community.

For Dr. Bethune, faith gives life a deep sense of purpose, enabling
the moral agent to become "doers of the word" of God and not hear-
ers only. Faith gives to each person or moral agent, a sense of *belonging*.
Theologically, we are called by God to be in relationship, to build up one
another in love, to pray together, to suffer together, and to overcome adversity together. Hence, the church that dares to be faithful to a freeing
and unfailing God, a God of liberation and the "healing of the land" (2
Chr 7:14; 2 Kgs 20:8), calls us not just to believe but also to belong. As
Holy Scripture clearly affirms: "You are members of God's very own family, citizens of God's country, and you belong in God's household with
every other Christian" (Eph 2:19). Now in the rhythmic flux of black life
in America, it was crystal clear to most of her contemporaries that Dr.
Mary McLeod Bethune knew well the difference between simply "believ-
ing" and the term "*belonging*." For the church of the living God, the latter
implies covenantal partnership in the body of Christ. The Bible says, "For
sin pays a wage . . . but God gives freely, and his gift is eternal life, in union
with Christ Jesus our Lord" (Rom 6:23). In the final analysis, Dr. Mary

McLeod Bethune could (look at life through the eyes of faith that it was the power of prayer and faith that she saw more than a dumping pile, she saw the virtuous school, prayer was the anchor.) source out of footnote 9 therefore say: " . . . through the eyes of faith I saw more than a city dumping pile . . . I saw the seeds of a virtuous school . . . beginning literally only with pennies . . . but anchored in the Power of Prayer."[34] Ethically and theologically considered, we wish to conclude our reflections in this chapter by looking, briefly, at a provocative case study entitled, "Hidden Fears."

First of all, I think that pastors, counselors, and Christian educators in the contemporary church must grapple with the sorts of issues raised in this particular case—as people's lives are torn apart. Ethically, no matter how perfect we as Christians, or non-Christians alike, attempt to live our lives, the human being is not immune to suffering and disappointment. Secondly, there are many complex issues and moral questions at stake in this case. For some, it is not primarily a case about "morality" versus "immorality," given the bittersweet pitfalls of marriage in contemporary society. However, I do hold the view—normatively discerned—that marital fidelity is integral to basic Christian values and family life in the black community. Thirdly, to some degree, the reader may be drawn from a *womanist* perspective, to examine the question of the dominance of black men over black women. Notwithstanding, I suspect for practical discussion, the dominant prevailing issues at stake in this case may well revolve around problems of betrayal, deception, and emotional hurt on the part of Linda, the wife of Russell. After this brief glimpse, let us now read and explore the drama of the case itself.

Case Study: Hidden Fears

"Now explain this again, Russell," the counselor inquires. "Why did you choose to reveal to your wife, Linda, that you are a 'brother-on-the-down-low?'" "Because the Holy Spirit told me to," responds the 29-year-old fellow. "And how did the Holy Spirit tell you?" "He spoke to me. You know, I remember somewhere in the Good Book, God says . . . "I will pour out my spirit upon all flesh" (Joel 2:28) . . . and I know that all I am, is sinful flesh," lamented Russell. In the office of his trusted pastor, Rev. Samuel Henderson, Russell further sobbed: "I feel so guilty and ashamed about my behavior . . . Plus my wife has given me a threat that she may leave me . . . O God, what am I to do? How do I cope with the deep hidden fears inside of my soul as a Christian?"

The young married man in this story is Russell Gordon. He has been, seemingly, happily married to Linda, age 27, for four years and they are the proud parents of Russell, Jr., age 3, and Carla, age 1. In terms of religious and social background, Russell grew up on the rough streets of Harlem in New York City. He tells the story about what it was like to live in a rat-infested project, and to have enough *street smarts* to avoid and survive the daily realities of drugs and gang violence. Moreover, Russell was born into a household with two older sisters, Amanda and Trinetta, now ages 34 and 31. Russell's mother, Jo Ann Gordon, is a single parent who is a deeply devout Christian, attempting to raise her children based on the biblical principles of faith as well as the moral teachings of Christ. During the children's formative years, the Gordon family attended a local neighborhood congregation by the name of St. Luke African Methodist Episcopal (A.M.E.) Church. Because of economic scarcity, Miss Gordon could not afford to send her children to college.

However, young Russell was gifted in music and upon his graduation from Booker T. Washington High School in Harlem, won a full-tuition scholarship in the field of music to Bethune-Cookman College in Daytona Beach. Later Russell recalled joyfully saying:

> "What a mighty God we serve, what an unexpected blessing from Jesus . . . I never thought I would ever go . . . yet I know that my mother's dream was that . . . someone in our family would one day attend college . . . I just never thought it would be me."

Comparatively, Linda Baker hails from Chicago. She grew up in a middle class family, a family that stressed the values of faith, self-integrity, and hard work. Inevitably, the social pathways of Russell and Linda crossed in the closely knitted campus community of Bethune-Cookman. Romantically, their social chemistry connected. They became friends. They fell in love. They eventually got married and had a family. Before graduating from college, Russell majored in music, with the occupational goal of becoming director of a band in the public school system of Daytona Beach. On the other hand, Linda, his wife, majored in secondary education and became a successful English teacher in a local private school.

As a young family, Russell and Linda are faithful members of St. Paul A.M.E. Church, Daytona Beach, where Rev. Samuel Henderson is senior pastor. Indeed, Russell has been active in the male chorus for at least three years. However until recently, he has been keeping this "dark secret" from his devoted wife, namely: "Russell is having an affair outside of marriage, and it is with another man!" Hence, the phrase, "brother-on-the-down-low" refers to this kind of sexual activity and marital infidelity. As a counselor, Pastor Henderson wants to empathize with Russell's situation; but he also recognizes the hurt and anger that Linda must be feeling deep inside of her own soul as this *bucket of mud* was thrown in her lap. Once Linda was initially told about the outside affair, she strongly shouted: "Russell . . . how could you stoop so low . . . to betray your marriage vows, especially with another man . . . apparently right under my nose . . . I don't know if I can ever forgive you." Meanwhile, Pastor Henderson tries to encourage Linda and Russell to hold on to their marriage—at least for the sake of the children. But Pastor Henderson, in a stoic moment of candor, admits to Russell that he's not sure if this relationship can be saved. Finally, Russell retorts, "I'm still trusting the Holy Spirit and the Lord to provide for me."

Ethical Approach

1. How are you going to handle Russell's view of the doctrine of the Holy Spirit?

2. Is it better to deal with doctrinal matters (See Joel 2:28; Gal 5:22–23), or to look for what may be going on in Russell's head and heart?

3. As a counselor or friend, what are some of the problems that are likely to be involved in this case?

4. What are the "hidden fears" and realities that Linda and Russell must face?

5. What *approach* would Jesus of Nazareth likely take?

Issues for Study and Discussion

1. What can be done to help Linda cope with her obvious hurt, anger, and pain? (See Isa 40:29; Ps 16:8, 33:20)

2. Is Russell coming clean regarding the seriousness of this outside affair? (See Ps 31:14–15; Eph 6:73; Gal 6:7)

3. How would you deal with the general issue of marital infidelity—especially confronting a "brother-on-the-down-low"? (See 2 Chr 15:7; Jer 33:3)

4. What is at stake for the children in this strained marriage? (See 1 Pet 4:7; Rom 8:28; Prov 7:1–20)

5. As a people tainted by sin, what is the pleasing thing to do in the eyes of God? (See Mic 6:8)

6. Is there a biblical basis for healing and forgiveness in this marital dilemma? (See Luke 23:32–34; Matt 6:12–14; Mark 11:26)

Notes

1. Rackham Holt, *Mary McLeod Bethune: A Biography* (New York: Doubleday & Co., Inc., 1964) 1. As a Christian ethicist, I am deeply concerned about the future direction of the contemporary black church today. It seems to me, at times, that many religious leaders, who seek to proclaim the word of God, have lost their moral nexus with the strong traditions that nurtured our existence as a people of African descent. Of course, one of those majestic and noble traditions is embodied in the life and work of Mary McLeod Bethune. Accordingly, I became fascinated with the scope of her great work during a recent sabbatical leave from Eden Theological Seminary, where I currently serve as the United Church Professor of Theology and History, St. Louis, Missouri. Through the assistance and kindness of President Oswald Bronson, I was a resident fellow on the historic campus of Bethune-Cookman College, located in Daytona Beach, Florida. Here I had good access to the archives of Mary McLeod Bethune, which served as the background and religio-ethical framework for this chapter.

2. Ibid., 1–2. The heart of grandmother Sophia was filled with a sense of deep gratitude to God, and joy—running like a river on the inside of her—for what had been given to the marital covenant of Patsy and Sam McLeod. Apparently, this newborn was affirmed by neighbors and friends as "something special." Spiritually speaking, in the context of the black religious experience, it was not uncommon for elders of the church to testify publicly that God had placed God's own *mark* upon the life of an individual. Hence, "*where God guides, God always provides,*" quipped one old-time Baptist preacher. To be sure, grandmother Sophia was able, apparently, to discern in this particular grandchild, "a design of God." Romans 8:29 says, "God knew what he was doing from the very beginning. He decided from the outset to shape the lives of those who love him along the same lines as the life of his Son . . . "

3. Ibid., 2.

4. Ibid., 19.

5. Jesse Walter Dees, Jr., *The College Built on Prayer: Mary McLeod Bethune* (New York: Ganis and Harris, 1953) 12. Early in her social development, young Mary McLeod had a deep passion for education and learning. Born roughly a decade after the Emancipation Proclamation, blacks found it difficult to acquire civil and political rights and were reduced to a virtual status of peonage by the sharecrop system. Historians and Christian ethicists suggest, therefore, that education was the one area where blacks made some progress—with the establishment of black colleges in the post-slavery period. Here it is critical to point out to the ethically sensitive person that the persistent zeal for education was largely fueled in black churches through the south. Undoubtedly, Mary Jane McLeod, in her formative years, became a beneficiary of this progress and value that were placed on education. "Education remains the key to both economic and political empowerment," said Barbara Jordan—former U. S. Congressperson (D–Texas) —"and that is why the schools charged with educating African Americans have, perhaps, the greatest, the deepest challenge of all."

6. Albert J. Raboteau, *Slave Religion: The Invisible Institution in the Antebellum South* (New York: Oxford University Press, 1978) 239–241cf. Historians, theologians, and ethicists have pointed out for many decades that during the antebellum period it was literally against the law to "educate" or to teach a slave to read and write. Learning symbolized not only knowledge and intelligence, but the power of being, the right to self-

determination and freedom in a land that saw the slave simply as a piece of property or an object to be used and exploited. The great abolitionist Harriet Tubman tells the story of being born into slavery, and how she rebelled against a system of dehumanization and suffering. At one point on her journey of struggle and hope, Tubman retorted: "I grew up like a neglected weed, ignorant of liberty, having no experience of it. Now that I've been free, I know what a dreadful condition slavery is." By the same token, Mary McLeod Bethune knew how "dreadful" life can be without the light of education for each and every poor child growing up in the Deep South. For Bethune, without education, no one can truly sing the song of freedom.

7. Dees, 18cf.

8. Holt, 49.

9. Dees, 19–20. From a historical perspective, very few schools in the state of Florida were available for the education of "colored people" around the turn of the twentieth century. While black institutions of higher learning such as Lane College and Fisk University in Tennessee or Atlanta University and Morehouse College in Georgia had been established decades earlier—the great masses of children of African descent were not exposed to formal educational instruction. Through daily meditations, hard work, and courage, Mary McLeod Bethune was determined to correct this educational void for poor children in the national black community, but particularly in the state of Florida. One of the perceptive books dealing with the significance of culture and religio-ethical roots of developing youths is Janice E. Hale-Benson's *Black Children: Their Roots, Culture, and Learning Styles* (Baltimore: The Johns Hopkins University Press, 1982).

10. Ibid., 21.

11. Ibid., 22.

12. Ibid.

13. Ibid., 23.

14. Ibid., 24.

15. Brian Wren, *Education for Justice: Pedagogical Principles* (Maryknoll, New York.: Orbis Books, 1977) 7. It is my fundamental conviction that Christian ethics for the black church community in America must, necessarily, link "education" and the struggle for "justice" together—especially since African Americans and other people of color must do battle against the triadic evils of racism, sexism, and classism. Accordingly, there must be a community-based ethic that affirms the importance of "education for justice." At the most basic level for our children and young adults, Mrs. Bethune's philosophy advocated that justice means, "giving to each child his or her due . . . and the opportunity to realize one's potential." The renowned sociologist E. Franklin Frazier once remarked: "The Negro does not want love. He wants justice."

16. Dees, 26–27cf.

17. Ibid., 23.

18. Benson Ebinne, et al., *Collaboration: A Collection of Poems* (St. Louis: Rycraw Productions, 1991) 17.

19. Jan Johnson, *Mary Bethune and Her Somedays* (Minneapolis: Winston Press, Inc., 1979) 20–21.

20. Ibid. Against the religio-cultural background of this powerful story, Christian ethics for the contemporary black church raises the critical question: *How many roads must we travel to locate the "Miss Wilsons" who have an educational vision of the common*

good? Accordingly, some Christian social ethicists in contemporary tell is that *pleasure* (or the principle of hedonism) is symbolic of the common good. Others simply say—in the long philosophical tradition of Aristotle and Plato—that "happiness" is symbolic of the common good. But in the context of the ethics of Jesus, love is the principle that empowers the church to speak of a common good for children, youths, adults, and all humanity (Matt 22:37–40). Love is not static in our efforts to locate the "Miss Wilsons" in both church and society. Like young Mary Jane McLeod, their stories of outreach and love become our opportunities of educational achievement and community service.

21. Dees, 13.

22. Cited in Janet Cheatham Bell, *Famous Black Quotations* (Chicago: Sabart Publications, 1986) 50cf.

23. Robert Michael Franklin, *Liberating Visions: Human Fulfillment and Social Justice in African American Thought* (Minneapolis: Fortress Press, 1990) 19.

24. The Mary McLeod Bethune Foundation: Foundation Collection, Part 1, Archives: "Origins, Vicissitudes, and Prospects" (The Research Center: Bethune-Cookman College, Daytona Beach, Florida).

25. The Mary McLeod Bethune Foundation: Foundation Collection, Part 1, The Mary McLeod Bethune Papers (The Research Center: Bethune-Cookman College, Daytona Beach, Florida). In the critical philosophy of Mary McLeod Bethune, there existed a social ethic inclusive of both *cognitive* work and *physical* work. The relationship between the two elements is dynamic and creative. For Bethune, to place one over the other in one's social life is nothing less than philosophical elitism. Therefore, I suspect that for pastors, Christian educators, and lay leaders of the black church today, the key ethical phrase— "men and women who are not afraid and ashamed to work"—exhibits a voice of realism deeply rooted in biblical faith. For example, the Bible teaches the Christian believer that every individual, learned or unlearned, must "work out his own salvation with fear and trembling . . . " (Phil 2:12). Galatians 6:4 seems to put a unitive thread between "physical" and "cognitive" work by boldly declaring: "all must test their own work." For Bethune, the upshot of this scenario reads: "there is as much dignity in plowing the soil for food, as it is in doing research in a lab for a scientific breakthrough!"

26 Audrey T. McCluskey and Elaine M. Smith, eds., *Mary McLeod Bethune: Building a Better World* (Bloomington and Indianapolis: Indiana University Press, 1999) 13–14cf.

27. Clarence G. Newsome, "Mary McLeod Bethune in Religious Perspective: A Seminar Essay," unpublished dissertation, Duke University, 1982, 171.

28. Ibid., 172.

29. Ibid., 172cf.

30. The Mary McCleod Bethune Foundation: The Foundation Collection, Part 1, Archives: "How God Helps" (The Research Center: Bethune-Cookman College, Daytona Beach, Florida) 2.

31. Ibid., 3.

32. Ibid., 4.

33. The Mary McCleod Bethune Foundation: The Foundation Collection, Part 1, Archives: "My Faith and My Job" (The Research Center: Bethune-Cookman College, Daytona Beach, Florida) 2cf.

34. Dees, 19–20.

Chapter Three

Womanist Ethics with a Noble Beat
The Stories of Rosa Parks and Coretta Scott King

*Black women whose ancestors were brought to the United States begin-
ning in 1619 have lived through conditions of cruelty so horrible, so
bizarre, the women had to reinvent themselves.*

—Maya Angelou, 1928
Novelist and Poet

*This is our moment. I honestly wouldn't be anyone but a black woman in
America right now. I feel that this is our time to break new ground.*

—Halle Berry, 1968
Actor

IN THIS chapter we shall look at the legacy, values, vision, and faith
of two extraordinary American women of the twentieth century: Rosa
Parks and Coretta Scott King. We shall also take a candid look at the residual problem of sexism in the contemporary black church community,
through the use of a case study at the end of the chapter. As a way to *recall*
some of the significant contributions of the Civil Rights movement, I have
carefully designed a "worksheet" or "teaser test" for the ethically discerning reader. Here you can test your knowledge and use it as an educational
resource with friends or as a tool for small group discussion in local congregations and community organizations. At least, this is my hope for the
reader in this chapter.

The word *noble* intentionally appears in the chapter's title.
Etymologically, the term "noble" is derived from the Latin *nobilis*, which
literally means "well-known," "exalted rank," "high birth" or a "person
possessing excellent qualities." Ethically discerned, "nobility" obligates (*no-
blesse oblige*) certain persons of high esteem in one's standards of conduct.

Therefore, it is only a glimpse into the obvious to see that these womanist visionaries, Mary McLeod Bethune, Rosa Parks, and Coretta Scott King, have left a blazing trail of achievements for all of us to follow. As we grow older, often the people who morally and spiritually shape our lives are not only parents but also people we admire and with whom we share abstract connections. In large measure, Rosa Parks and Coretta Scott King fit into this existentialist category for me. Concretely, I never met Rosa Parks in the flesh; I did meet Coretta Scott King—as the drama of her powerful story unfolds later in this chapter.

Yet on my own ethical and spiritual journey, Rosa Parks and Coretta Scott King serve as *inspirational diamonds* that sparkled against the brutal darkness of fear and racial bigotry in our society. While neither, obviously, was a biological mother to me, I feel deep within my spirit that I have been influenced by their *mothering instinct* of love, and tough-minded passion for justice—in a so-called democratic society that pigeonholed young African American children as inferior. With these moral warriors and womanist icons in particular, I feel a connection because for some reason their stories have become embedded in our lives. Their stories are *our* story. Their struggles symbolized our striving. Their hurts became an instrument for our hope as Black people and White people, as Latinos and Asians, as Native Americans and other people of color gave of themselves for a higher ideal. As strong women of faith, their stories are interwoven like a vulnerable piece of clay in the hands of a Master Potter. They set the boundaries of ethical deliberation—not based on a slick Madison Avenue "image" but on moral action—in addressing some of the critical problems confronting African Americans in the mid-1950s and 1960s.

For example, in the book of Jeremiah, it is a peculiar sensation of ethical significance that God, the sovereign Lord of heaven and earth, is imaged as the Master Potter who can remake and transfigure all of our problems: spiritual, moral, economic, or multicultural. As women of faith, they both were "by-products" of the black religious experience in America. That's a beautiful thing in and of itself! Besides, in order for us to express personal integrity and accept social responsibility as children of God, Rosa Parks and Coretta Scott King believed that we must address the critical issues in our time. Undoubtedly, they both believed that God is present with us in the struggle for what is right. Existentially, this reality of God's presence that bears down upon our lives means that while we are trying to figure it out, often through the process of moral reasoning and self-examination, God has already worked it out!

In the drama of biblical faith, we may recall how God instructed the prophet Jeremiah to "go down to the potter's house" (Jer 18:1). Here, as the narrative unfolds, Jeremiah was found obedient to the divine imperative as he carefully observed the potter's choice of raw materials (i.e., broken vessels of clay), the sort of materials that nobody seems to want: abandoned stuff, spoiled stuff, and the "stuff" that needed to be "reworked" into another vessel (Jer 18:4). In white America of the 1950s, both Rosa Parks and Coretta Scott King painfully understood that black folk were regarded as second-class citizens, as the outcast, as the "nobodies," and as the "abandoned stuff." But the story does not end there in regard to the heart of the Master Potter. Accordingly, the intrinsic value in the legacy of both Rosa Parks and Coretta Scott King is the bold recognition that God can take a "nobody" and turn her or him into a "somebody!" God can take a *broken vessel* of disgrace and change it into a *glorious vessel* of amazing grace. God can take the heavy chains of unfreedom and transform them into the joyful bells of freedom. Against the fascinating drama of their committed lives, the terminology "womanist ethics with a new beat" best reflects what they were about—or so it seems to me.

To be quite candid, words like "womanist" and "womanism" did not appear in the regular patterns of Afrocentric language in the 1950s and 1960s, describing the interests, affairs, and experiences of black women. It really did not slip into the popular culture as well as into our academic lexicon until the mid-1980s—as black women writers in the disciplines of biblical studies, theology, and ethics began to find a new literary vehicle for self-expression. They did not necessarily use the *womanist vocabulary*, but their passion, action, and vision—from the progressive voice of Mary McLeod Bethune to the quiet strength of Coretta Scott King—reflected the core of the womanist identity. In the social struggle for racial justice, both believed that God is the power or revolutionary force that bears down upon us, re-molds, re-works, reshapes us; snatches our lives from the edges of destruction, and orders our footsteps in the path of truth. As Scripture clearly affirms for the Christian community: "I am the way, and the truth, and the life" (John 14:6). Along their ethical and spiritual journey therefore, these two womanist thinkers encouraged our youths, our elders, our church community, and our nation to "go down to the potter's house" and be made anew, as we together face the challenges of a new century. Metaphorically, these womanist thinkers knew deep within their souls, that it is only at the potter's house that we struggle, inevitably, with the deep moral questions, painful rejections, ambiguities, and the contradictions of historical existence. Since their lives represent a pivotal point in

America history, we shall provide the reader with a brief snapshot of their stories separately, in order to shed light on the rich legacy they left behind for all Americans and the world community to follow. However, before we attempt to engage the meaning of their legacies for us in human community, let us first take a brief look at the emergence of womanist ethics.

Functional Definition of Womanist Ethics

The term "womanist ethics" strikes the ear as an oxymoron. The chasms that stretch between the discipline of ethics and our ordinary lives of faith seem to exist, because our perspective of doing ethics in contemporary society does not appear to be anything other than *theoretical*. But I am here today to boldly declare that ethics is not only a matter of logic and theory, but life and struggle. Fundamentally, it is my moral conviction that both Rosa Parks and Coretta Scott King are pivotal examples of "womanist ethics" in the contemporary black church. Their lives reflect community-formed stories that dramatically impacted countless millions of people in this nation and around the world.

Pragmatically, their lessons of Christian humility encourage us to ask: what in the world is womanist ethics? Does it relate to a theology of *praxis*, reflective of the actual situations of suffering and oppressed people around the world? Concretely, how does it connect with the struggle of black people in America for authentic freedom and equality today? Is there a link between womanist ethics in the *pew* and male power in the *pulpit*? For both Mrs. Parks and Mrs. King, these are ethically serious questions. They are not only important concerns for African American Christians, but for anyone who has felt the pain of being the "last-hired-and-first-fired," of being the "disinherited" before we know what it means to speak of economic *inheritance*, of being the "locked-out" before we could fully grasp the politics of inclusion in the so-called *land of the free and home of the brave*!

Notwithstanding, in the 1950s and 1960s, faith-driven interpretations of meaning empowered women like Rosa Parks and Coretta Scott King to find a moral agenda in a white racist society that could advocate forgiveness and love over hatred and revenge—and especially, in the critical thought of Coretta Scott King (i.e., adapted, in part, from the theology of Martin Luther King, Jr.), the view that *suffering* itself is redemptive for the followers of Christ. Prior to the sixties, strong black women and black churches nurtured survival skills in the fields of education, politics, religion, economics, and sports, to name only a few.

However, in the waning years of the Civil Rights movement, the more radical voices of Black Nationalism and black struggle began to challenge the traditional pastoral practices and "centers of power" in the wider community. In challenging the traditional pastoral practices and obscure roles of women, it is easy to point out that the militancy of the black power movement in the late sixties is a case in point. Any cursory literary glance at the post-Civil Rights era of the sixties reveals a subtle paradigm shift in the social analysis of the situation from idyllic integration to constructive liberation. A selected litany of books seems to reflect, in part, this paradigm shift, including: *Arise, Awake, Act: A Womanist Call for Black Liberation*, by Marcia Riggs; *In Search of Our Mothers' Gardens*, by Alice Walker; *Daughters of the Dust*, by Julie Dash; *Black Religion*, by Joseph R. Washington, Jr.; *Dark Ghetto*, by Kenneth B. Clark; *The Black Messiah*, by Albert B. Cleage, Jr.; *Black Power: The Politics of Liberation in America*, by Stokely Carmichael, et al; and *Black History Reappraisal*, by Melvin Drimmer, ed. This highly selective list reflects, in part, the ongoing issues, debates, and conflicting perspectives peculiar to black Christians as we face a new future. The crucial variables that will, undoubtedly, shape the black community's future are not always crystal clear. But what is clear, in my own ethical thinking, arises from the fact that the "womanist-mystique" of Rosa Parks and Coretta Scott King symbolize a *womanist-ethics in a new beat*. What, then, is the source of the term "womanist?" Ethymologically, the term "womanist" was coined by Pulitzer prize-winning novelist Alice Walker in her classic work *In Search of Our Mothers' Gardens*, in 1983. The use of the term literally means a woman who is "sassy," "womanish," "morally defiant," "courageous," and "audacious." In the book *Living The Intersection: Womanism and Afrocentrism in Theology*, the authors Kelly Brown Douglas and Cheryl J. Sanders say that, "African American women have adopted the term as a symbol of their experience. *Womanist* signals an appreciation for the richness, complexity, uniqueness, and struggle involved in being black and female in society that is hostile to both blackness and womanhood."[1] The terms *womanist ethics* or *womanist* are descriptive of the spirit and moral vitality of both Rosa Parks and Coretta Scott King. The core values and ethical principles inherent in their lives demonstrated the breadth and depth of womanism in the contemporary black community. Accordingly, I strongly believe that womanist ethics wrestles with the meaning and purpose of life, as seen through the concrete lens of women's experiences—their hopes and heartaches, and their faith and vision for a better world. For both God-talk and God-walk, it is the lived world of experience that makes a difference. At a brief glance, the womanist ethical perspective challenges us to broaden our viewpoint of what is going on around us. Hence, the spirit of womanism boldly claims:

> Womanist scholarship gives expression to African American women's efforts—political, cultural, emotional, psychological, spiritual—to resist the "interlocking system" of multiple oppression, i.e., racism, sexism, and classism, that would thwart the life and well-being of African American women and men as well as girls and boys. The womanist perspective, therefore, involves mining the culture and history of African American women in an effort to forge a way of living that fosters life and wholeness for the African American community.[2]

A Black Woman's Seat, Segregation's Defeat!

On December 1, 1955, the grace and poise of an obscure attractive woman, Rosa Parks, boarded a Montgomery, Alabama city bus and took a "white only" restrictive seat; and this solitary act of courage, inevitably, led to segregation's defeat. In a single sentence, the rest is commentary. The rest is history. The rest is legacy. The rest is the "things" legends are made of. The rest is moral tradition peculiar to the struggles of African American people living in America. The rest is a formative source in understanding the importance of womanist ethics in a new beat. However, the perilous details of Rosa Parks's extraordinary story reflect something like the leaves from the diary of a Greek Olympian destined for victory, by any means necessary, being, as it were, favored by the God of history.

With skillful hands and sharp minds, black women like Rosa Parks had worked in many white department stores in cities throughout the South. So then, Thursday, December 1, 1955 had been a busy day for Mrs. Raymond A. Parks. Her official job title was that of a tailor's assistant at the Montgomery Fair Department store. On this day, as was her custom, she left work at 5:30 p.m. and went to her usual bus stop on Court Square. As the cold December weather touched the darkness of evening, Mrs. Parks observed that the buses were especially crowded as she waited and eventually boarded one for her Cleveland Avenue route.[3] Having boarded the 1948 General Motors bus, only one row of seats, the row immediately behind the first ten seats reserved by law for whites only, had any vacancies. Here Mrs. Parks took an aisle seat, with a black man on her right side next to the window, and two black women in the parallel seats across the way.[4]

As the bus continued to pick up passengers at the next two stops, African Americans moved further to the rear of the bus in order to allow whites to occupy their exclusive seats at the front of the bus. In this system of *de jure* segregation, whites always had first claim and first choice. At the third stop along the route—in this peculiar system of white privilege—we observe that more passengers got on, and one, a white male, was left standing after the final front seat was taken. Now for the traditional power brokers of southern culture that was a big "No" "No!" That is to say: "No white man should be left standing . . . while a black person is comfortably seated on any bus in America." Immediately, the bus driver, J. F. Blake, looked in the direction of Mrs. Parks and her three colleagues and loudly barked: "All right you folks, I want those two seats."[5] Tension and silence gripped the social atmosphere in the bus, but nobody moved. Then Blake spoke out again: "you all better make it light on yourselves and let me have those seats."[6] At that point, two women across from Mrs. Parks anxiously rose to their feet and moved to the rear. For whatever reasons, the man beside her rose also, and inevitably, moved to the back of the bus. Rosa Parks remained stubbornly silent but, shifted to the window side of the seat—as if to say: "I have a right to sit wherever I choose as any other American citizen!" But J. F. Blake could clearly see that Mrs. Parks still had not gotten up. Perhaps in a flash of anger, he muttered: "Look woman, I told you I wanted the seat. Are you going to stand up?"[7] At that time, Rosa Lee McCauley Parks was willing to go the second mile to put a nail in the coffin of segregation as she muttered her first word to him: "No." This was the revolutionary "No!" that was heard around the world, and served as a moral force for the good. Immediately, J. F. Blake responded in a way consistent with the traditions and customs of southern white society: "If you don't stand up, I'm going to have you arrested."[8] Mrs. Parks was familiar with the nitty-gritty details of the routine in moral defiance of a system of segregation. The routine was this: Blake got off the bus and came back a few minutes later with two police officers. Rosa Parks was, then, carried to the station, fingerprinted and booked in 1955 after refusing to give up her seat on a bus to a white man in Montgomery, Alabama.

Word of Mrs. Parks's arrest began to spread like wildfire throughout the Montgomery black community. One morally concerned passenger on the 1948 General Motors bus told a friend about Mrs. Parks's ordeal, and that friend, Mrs. Bertha Butler, immediately called the home of Rev. E. D. Nixon, a social activist and Past President of Montgomery's National Association for the Advancement of Colored People (NAACP). It was Nixon, along with Clifford Durr, a liberal white lawyer, who actually went down and signed the $100 bond to secure the release of Mrs. Rosa Parks from jail. Symbolically and contextually, Mrs. Parks's immediate Civil Rights posse included: Fred Gray, Montgomery's principle black lawyer; Rev. H. H. Hubbard, President of the Baptist Ministerial Alliance; Rev. L. Roy Bennett, President of the Interdenominational Ministerial Alliance; Mrs. A. W. West, the widow of a prominent local dentist; Rev. Ralph Abernathy, the young minister of Montgomery's First Baptist Church; Mrs. Jo Ann Robinson, President of the Women's Political Council (WPC) and community activist for quality education; and Rev. Martin Luther King, Jr., pastor of Dexter Avenue Baptist Church, to name only a few. Now following this pivotal incident of Rosa Parks, the dominant sentiment in Montgomery's black community was this: "We're tired of taking the insults of segregation and mistreatment . . . and we ain't gonna take it no more!" E. D. Nixon, the signer of the bond for the 42-year-old seamstress, described the demoralizing incident in a way that resembles a biblical prophet as well as a contemporary pragmatist. He proclaimed:

> We have taken this type of thing too long already . . . I feel that the time has come to boycott the buses. Only through a boycott can we make it clear to white folks that we will not accept this type of treatment any longer.[9]

This simple act of courage placed her in high esteem of countless millions of people around the world and earned her the affectionate title of "Mother of the Civil Rights Movement." Reflecting on the collective struggle of black people, A. Philip Randolph, the great labor leader and economic strategist, once remarked: "there are no *free seats* at the table of life. All seats must be struggled for and taken." For example, in his classic book *Strife Toward Freedom*, Martin Luther King, Jr., recalls the story of the quiet courage of Rosa Parks in these decisive words:

> Tired from long hours on her feet, Mrs. Parks sat down in the first seat behind the section reserved for whites. Not long after she took her seat, the bus operator ordered her, along with three other Negro passengers, to move back in order to accommodate boarding white passengers. By this time every seat in the bus was taken. This meant that if Mrs. Parks followed the driver's command she would have to stand while a white male passenger, who had just boarded the bus, would sit. The other three Negro passengers immediately complied with the driver's request. But Mrs. Parks quietly refused. The result was her arrest.[10]

Moreover, King goes on to suggest that there were many people in the local white community of Montgomery who speculated that Mrs. Parks had intentionally been "planted" by the N A A C P to stage this dramatic incident in order to lay the groundwork for a test case for ending segregation in America's public life. Certain journalists and reporters in the national media raised the cynical question: Did the NAACP, behind the scenes, start the wheels rolling for a massive bus boycott in Montgomery? To this critical question, King and his contemporary advocates for the Civil Rights movement responded with a resounding "No!" The charge and accusations were false. As a champion of freedom and justice Martin Luther King, Jr., puts the matter succinctly:

> . . . the accusation was totally unwarranted, as the testimony of both Mrs. Parks and the officials of the NAACP revealed. Actually, no one can understand the action of Mrs. Parks unless he realizes that eventually the cup of endurance runs over, and the human personality cries out, "I can take it no longer." Mrs. Parks's refusal to move back was her intrepid affirmation that she had had enough. It was an individual expression of a timeless longing for human dignity and freedom. She was not "planted" there by the NAACP, or any other organization; she was planted there by her personal sense of dignity and self-respect. She was anchored to that seat by the accumulated indignities of days gone by and the boundless aspirations o generations yet unborn. She was a victim of both the forces of history and the forces of destiny. She had been tracked down by the Zeitgeist—the spirit of the time.[11]

Faith as the Glass Half Full

The legacy of Rosa Parks incorporates and ethically reflects the spirit of the *Zeitgeist*, as an American woman who refused to bow down to the pharaoh of white supremacy. The spiritual legacy of Rosa Parks teaches us that we, in fact, can choose to see the glass as "half empty" or "half full." As moral agents, the choice is up to us. But faith, in the *oral tradition* of our wise elders and African ancestors, seems to move in the direction of seeing the glass "half full" despite the pain, suffering, and tribulations of life.

For example, in Kenya of East Africa, there is a large ethnic group known as the Kykuyu. Here the Kykuyu folks have a popular saying: "faith knows the truth in one's heart, before the eyes can see." Accordingly, Mrs. Parks, as a woman of faith, had a vision anchored deep within her heart, that what was hoped for would one day come to pass.

"All I have seen teaches me to trust the Creator for all I have not seen," echoed the poet Ralph Waldo Emerson. Fundamentally, it is no accident therefore, that faithfulness is the central theme in the biblical story of the Hebrew people seeking deliverance from oppression and "the house of slavery" (Ex 20:1–21; Deut 7:7–11; Ps 27:1–5). For Rosa Parks, faith is the secret weapon for every battle; it is the key that unlocks every door as Blacks, Latinos, Asians, Native Americans, and other people of color struggle for authentic freedom and justice in America. Faith means seeing the glass "half full" rather than "half empty" with the blessed assurance that victory is on the way. As Holy Scripture affirms " . . . and this is the victory that overcometh the world, even our faith" (1 John 5:4).

For Rosa Parks, faith not only links us to salvation in the "after-life," but liberation in "this life." Faith clothes us in the power and strength of the Divine. Faith links us to the untamed path of the *Zeitgeist*.[12] Faith insures us that every attribute of who God is serves in our defense and struggle for human dignity and equality. Faith, at its best, gives the moral agent or Christian believer both roots and wings. In the former sense, there is an old gospel song expressive of this deep spiritual *root*, namely, "*My Soul is Anchored in the Lord*." The latter is profoundly reflected, I think, in the poetic dictum often muttered by the elders of the Afrocentric *oral tradition*: "young brothers and sisters . . . don't forget to keep your eyes on the prize; although you can't see clearly the bumps in the road ahead of you . . . or the fierce and measured resistance to your struggle . . . just keep *pressing toward the mark*." Be that as it may, I strongly believe and evidence suggests, that Mrs. Rosa Parks always attempted to see the glass "half full" rather than "half empty"—as she was a covenantal by-product of the *Zeistgeist*.

Of course, the wind of the *Zeistgeist*—like the decisive hands of God—caught this impeccable woman of character by surprise. No one chooses to be a centering moment for history's favor or disfavor. No one chooses to be a "rose" because realists of the womanist persuasion, all too well, know that "thorns" come along with the roses. No one chooses to intentionally fall on her or his sword, as an act of valor—while the steep walls of racial segregation must be climbed. So then, the humiliating incident suffered by Mrs. Rosa Parks was unplanned, unrehearsed. There was no tactical "wizard of Oz" that conjured up a suitable person with a suitable scheme to contest the traditional bus segregation laws in the Deep South. Somehow, I cannot help but believe that God was in the plan, from the beginning, guiding the courageous action and finite rhythms of Rosa Parks, on that unforgettable Thursday evening (December 1, 1955), around 5:30 p.m. as she boarded the Cleveland Avenue bus in downtown Montgomery. There is, I think, an African American proverb that reads: "Where God guides, God always provides!"

Accordingly, Rosa Parks was "guided" to resist the injustice of segregation in American society and to rebel against those who would be prone to mistreat her based on skin-color. Here, I am reminded of the profound wisdom often articulated by Dr. Benjamin E. Mays, former President of Morehouse College (Atlanta, Georgia), to his students on campus:

> Fleecy locks and dark complexion cannot forfeit nature's claim;
> skin may differ, but intellect and affection run in black and white
> the same.[13]

Symbolically and contextually Rosa Parks's immediate Civil Right's posse after this historic incident supported her in an understanding of faith as seeing the glass *half full*—despite the difficulty in the collective struggle for a new social order reflective of freedom, racial equality, and the concrete dismantling of the laws of segregation. Faith is never easy when it has to be tested. Parks's faith was tested every day in the fires of racial insults, indignities, and a loathing intensity for people of African descent. As the African proverb so eloquently puts it: "only those who have been tried in the fire, will not scorch in the sun."

Undoubtedly, her faith has been tried in the fire; but faith itself is not the absence of doubt—rather the absence of fear. Here in the critical thought of Rosa Parks, there was, apparently, never a "fear" of J. F. Blake or a "fear" of losing her $23 per week job as a seamstress at the Fair Department Store in downtown Montgomery. Perhaps the only "fear" arose from the potentiality of losing her God-given dignity, and being regarded forever by whites as a "nigger" in the throes of a segregationist system. Herbert Kohl's perceptive work *She Would Not Be Moved*, suggests to us that this was precisely the truth inherent in the story of Rosa Parks and the Montgomery Bus Boycott. He makes his case with this quotation from Robert Fulgham, who asserts:

> Rosa Parks. Not an activist or a radical. Just a quiet, conservative, churchgoing woman with a nice family and a decent job as a seamstress. For all the eloquent phrases that have been turned about her place in the flow of history, she did not get on that bus looking for trouble or trying to make a statement. Going home was all she had in mind, like everybody else. She was anchored to her seat by her own dignity. Rosa Parks simply wasn't going to be a "nigger" for anybody anymore. And all she knew to do was to sit still.[14]

Thus, in the critical thought of Rosa Parks, faith seeks understanding—an understanding that critiques all patterns of Jim Crowism and niggerism in our national life. In my own volume, *O Lord Move This Mountain: Racism and Christian Ethics*, I argue that to be morally honest, if we say that racism is wrong for America, that racism is destructive to our health and wellness, then we must also say that "niggerism" is wrong for the black community.[15] Why do black people, occasionally, call *each other* niggers? For example, when I first went to Africa—during a sabbatical leave from Eden Seminary, St. Louis, Missouri—to teach and to learn from indigenous people of faith, the main thing I observed arises from the fact that I never heard *anybody* call each other a "nigger!" Unfortunately, some young brothers of the hip-hop culture in America try and "market" this idolatrous self-loathing word as a *term of endearment*. To this social myth, the womanist ethic and faith of Rosa Parks responds with a resounding "No!" She said "no" to the psychological injury caused by this word in the social development of our children in the national black community. On this point of the complexity of faith as seeing the glass "half full," there is a growing awareness that the subtle issues are beyond the narrow boundaries of the black-white dilemma. In the language of Carter G. Woodson, the prevailing moral dilemma is the "mis-education of *both* the African American and the European American." Therefore, faith is active as we see it as a symbol of the glass being half full. Faith that is real—in the legacy of Rosa Parks—works on behalf of the common good. Moral struggle and faith cannot be easily separated. They are integral to our understanding of human community. Therefore, work and faith belong together. Listen here to the Letter of James:

> Can faith save you? If a brother or sister is naked and lacks daily food, and one of you says to them, "Go in peace, keep warm and eat your fill," and yet you do not supply their bodily needs, what is the good of that? So faith by itself, if it has no works, is dead. But someone will say "You have faith and I have works" show me your faith apart from your works, and I by my works will show you my faith (Jas 2:14–18).

For Rosa Parks, the turbulent years of the mid–1950s could not have been endured apart from the dynamic works of faith. Every warrior who sets out upon a journey must have faith that she or he will succeed. And the Christian narrative reminds us all that "failure" is not final. I remember in the community of my childhood growing up in Earle, Arkansas, my 98-year-old grandpa telling me: "Bud . . . my grandson, I wanna tell you something you must never forget as a black boy of the South . . . that is to say . . . on the road to freedom, you can't fly, if you're afraid to fail." Accordingly, those words of wisdom are lodged within my heart from my grandpa; and they remind me of Rosa Parks's bold faith and courage. At every point in life, faith is always seeking greater understanding of the human condition.

From the perspective of ethnicity and theology, faith is the condition of being ultimately concerned about what is going on in our world. For Parks, it certainly has to do with understanding and grasping the critical moral and racial issues at stake in America. In the language of Paul Tillich, faith has not only to do with *grasping of* but being *grasped by* the love and grace of God. The metaphor of the glass being "half full" is a narrative way of affirming, as the people of God, the interrelatedness of all that is. Faith is a way, for better or worse, of seeing the "end" (i.e., *de jure* segregation) of something before it takes place. Accordingly, Rosa Parks and her contemporaries saw—through the eyes of faith—a day in our nation when we would no longer have humiliating signs in the arena of our public life that read: "Whites only," "Colored only," "Niggers stay away!" "No coons allowed!" For Mrs. Parks, faith is the wisdom not to be bound in one's soul by these negative racial stereotypes so peculiar to the decades of the 1940s and 1950s.

In short, we may say that faith as reflected in the legacy of Rosa Parks resembled what some medieval thinkers called the "beatific vision"—seeing the ultimate no longer "through a glass darkly but face-to-face." Jesus said, "According to your faith will it be done to you (Matt 9:29). One translation simply reads: "Have what your faith expects." Rosa Parks *expected* equal treatment in a society that had denied her first class citizenship based on the color of one's skin; and Rosa Parks prayed as she expected great things from God, by attempting great things for God. Historical records show that she never went around feeling victimized by the *poor-little-me mentality* or complaining: "*O Lord, I feel so depressed because life is not fair!*" Rather, the totality of her legacy reflects a "glass half-full" person in the struggle to eliminate racial segregation in the Deep South. As a Christian, she not only embraced the notion that prayer gives the believer strength for the journey, but that prayer itself changes things. There is a tremendous harvest in one's life when we know the power of prayer. "I pray also . . . that you may know the hope to which he has called you, the riches of his glorious inheritance in the saints, and his incomparably great power for us who believe" (Eph 1:18–19).

Who, after all, is this famous woman the world has come to know as Rosa Parks? Well, history is always partial to irony and surprise. It has been said and some believe that nobody knows exactly where in Tuskegee, Alabama, Rosa McCauley was born on February 4, 1913. Moreover, the local town newspaper reported that the skies were bright and clear and it was unseasonably warm that day, but beyond that, and the fact that she was named after her maternal grandmother, Rose, virtually no reliable documentation exists on the early years of Rosa Louise Parks.[16]

In the traditional stroll down memory lane, native Tuskegeeians are quick to point with a sense of *Hollywood pride* to their own stars and African American heroes, from Booker T. Washington to George Washington Carver, from Ralph Ellison to Lionel Richie and the Commodores. Parenthetically, one of our sons had the privilege of attending Tuskegee University, indeed, one of the great black institutions of higher learning in our nation. In the perceptive work *Rosa Parks, A Life*, Douglas Brinkley carefully describes the formative years of young Rosa Parks, in terms of the impact of the black religious community upon her own consciousness. He wrote:

> Even as a dreamy, mild-mannered young girl, Rosa McCauley had found the black pulpit intoxicating in the openness it accorded preachers to weave the joyous exaltations and heartrending laments that were legacies of the West African culture passed down from generations of slaves to the sharecroppers of 1920s Alabama. "The church, with its musical rhythms and echoes of Africa, thrilled me when I was young," Parks recalled.[17]

In the *oral* tradition of the black church, Rosa Parks grew up with such Christian hymns as *"Steal Away to Jesus," "Joshua Fit the Battle of Jericho,"* and *"Woke up This Morning with my Mind Stayed on Jesus."* Any causal glance at history suggests that struggle and resistance have marked the morally conflicted story of Africans brought to America from the beginning of their enslavement. Africans were forced away from their homes to labor, in the heat of the day, in service of Europeans in a society that prided itself in its commitments to the Christian ideals of brotherhood, freedom, and equality. Of course, the moral contradictions inherent in our society were tested time and again by Rosa Parks and other persons of color.

Fundamentally, the followers of Christ are set free by their faith. For Rosa Parks, Christian faith did not mean slavery. It meant freedom! It was this same interpretation of "Christian faith" that southern white landowners tried to hide from blacks. Tiptoeing through the pages of history, Douglas Brinkley makes this sobering observation:

> For a long time Southern whites hadn't wanted blacks to become Christians, preferring to pretend that slaves had no souls. From 1619, when the first human captives landed in Virginia, until 1773 there were no black churches anywhere in America, and the only blacks in white churches were relegated to the galleries. But from the Revolutionary War era onward, African Americans took not only the Bible but organized religious gatherings and rituals as passionately to heart as their ancestors had those of their native African faiths, such as the Yoruba religion, whose adherents memorized thousands of proverbs and allegories.[18]

Since early childhood in the rural outskirts of Montgomery—a place where she learned Bible passages by heart—Parks had been a faithful worker in the African Methodist Episcopal Church. Richard Allen founded this religious institution in 1816 in Philadelphia, Pennsylvania. During the stony road of the Abolitionist Movement, the A.M.E. Church was known as the "freedom church." Because of patterns of cultural racism in America, the historic A.M.E. Church had broken away from the white Methodist mainstream that condoned slavery. In short, Stewart Burns, in his insightful book *To The Mountaintop*, observes the following: "The A.M.E., less patriarchal than black Baptists, had always had a majority of female members, who like Parks, were its informal leaders. Women A.M.E. preachers had been prominent for a century, although not ordained until 1948.[19]

Listen to the Voices of Children and Young People

We begin this section with a pivotal question, namely: What words are worth listening to and passing on from elders to our children and youth today? In the fiery furnace of Jim Crowism, Parks recalled her grandfather once saying, "you don't put up with bad treatment from anybody . . . it was passed down almost in our genes."[20] Kevin Chappell's groundbreaking essay, *"The Life and Legacy of The Mother of The Civil Rights Movement,"* argues that blacks in Montgomery in the mid-1950s had made up their minds that they weren't going to get on the bus until Jim Crow got off.[21]

Shortly after the Montgomery Bus Boycott had successfully ended roughly a year later, both Mrs. Rosa Parks and her husband Raymond Parks lost their local jobs, and eventually moved to Detroit. Like Martin and Coretta, they, too, had received numerous death threats. "For the next eight years," says Chappell, "they lived an uneventful life. She struggled to find regular work, even moving to Virginia for a short time to work at Hampton College."[22] Among the oral stories of the black church tradition, there is a popular saying: "Where there is a will, there is a way!" Undoubtedly, Rosa Parks always had the will and courage to stand up for what is right; and in 1965, the newly elected U.S. Representative John Conyers (D-Mich.) hired Parks to work for him in his Detroit office. By the way, Rep. Conyers referred to her as his "celebrity staffer!" Civil rights activist Andrew Young believed that it was the "purity of her character" that galvanized the Freedom Movement in Montgomery and beyond, and made ordinary people of African descent feel that, if "they" (whites) could throw Parks in jail, then no one was safe. Reflecting on the life and legacy of the "Mother of the Civil Rights Movement," U. S. Senator Barack Obama (D-Ill.) boldly observed:

> Parks's "gaze is one of a woman who was not looking for trouble the day she refused to give up her seat; one who was not planning to get arrested . . . In her eyes, you see a woman who was ready for the choice she made. One who, when confronted with a decision that could have meant physical harm and certainly meant the loss of her own freedom, was prepared to accept all consequences in the name of what was right—of what was true."[23]

Besides her obvious love of freedom and equality, Rosa Parks had a passion for children and the future youth of America. She advocated for the power of their potential. Like countless women of valor of her generation, such as Jo Ann Robinson, Fannie Lou Hamer, Mae Bertha Carter, Diane Nash, Dr. Dorothy Height, to name only a few, Rosa Parks was strong in her belief of empowering young people to find their own voice. In the introduction to the volume *She Would Not Be Moved*, Marian Wright Edelman makes this cogently relevant point concerning Rosa Parks's passion and love of children, in light of their own potentiality:

> Putting Mrs. Parks's story in its full context allows children to get a much fuller sense of the kinds of planned activism and community action that happened in small towns and larger cities across the South during the Civil Rights movement. It's important for them to know that courageous leaders like Rosa Parks and Martin Luther King Jr., didn't suddenly appear out of nowhere, and that they weren't superhumans with magical powers. They were ordinary people, just like all of the other parents, neighbors, and ministers in the community, and like all of the familiar adults in our children's lives today. But they became heroes and made his-

tory because they were willing to stand up and make a difference. Teaching children this lesson reinforces the idea that *they* can make a difference too.[24]

The key role children and young adults have played in the Freedom Movement has been nothing less than remarkable—from the "Little Rock Nine" integrated into public education to the "sit-ins" at lunch counters in the Deep South, from "pray-ins" in Selma to moral rebellion against the fire hoses in Birmingham. With their idealism and vulnerability, children of color have been on the firing line in the struggle to eradicate racial bigotry and injustice in America. Perhaps one of the main lessons adults can learn from children is simple as it is awesome: *listen to the voices of children and young folks; give them space to speak and respond to our stuff.* Our children and young folks don't need, I think, Draconian drill sergeants but compassionated coaches who will lead by example and moral encouragement. Undoubtedly, a main lesson that children can learn from their elders is this: *stand-up for what is right, love God, respect yourself and everyone you meet, and never let go of your dreams.* In a nutshell, the beautiful stories in American history, to paraphrase Marian Wright Edelman, remind our children and adolescents that, "you are never too young to make a difference." Accordingly in 1987, ten years after her husband's death, Mrs. Parks founded the Rosa and Raymond Parks Institute for Self-Development as a lasting symbol of her work and love for children. "Since then" said Chappell, "more than 7,000 youth have benefited from the institute that mentors students and teaches them about their history."[25]

I am convinced that through the simple act of listening we become more fully human. Why not, then, listen to the voices of our children? They may be trying to tell us something worth paying attention to. How can we not fail to embrace Jesus' own moral injunction and imperative to his followers regarding children:

> They brought children for him to lay his hands on them with prayer. The disciples rebuked them, but Jesus said to them, 'Let the children come to me; do not try to stop them; for the kingdom of Heaven belongs to such as these.' And he laid his hands on the children and went his way. (Matt 19:13–15 NEB)

Marian Wright Edelman makes this insightful summary comment in regard to the life and legacy of Rosa Parks. Here she emphatically proclaimed:

> It's also crucial for our children to learn that Rosa Parks was a strong woman with a plan to fight for what she believed in so that both boys and girls will understand she is part of a rich history of

women's activism. Even today, sometimes we still need to remind our children that not all of the heroes of American history are white or male. And in every major American and progressive political social reform movement, women have always played a critical role. Many times they are in the background, employing quiet leadership and organizational, communication, and fundraising skills—but often they are at the forefront, acting as the catalyst for progress when it needs to happen. The quest for a better world has been, and is, the daily work of thousands upon thousands of women everywhere.[26]

I want to bring closure to this section of the chapter on the rich legacy of Rosa Parks by sharing with you a true personal story of what it was like for me growing up as an African American child in the state of Arkansas—struggling with issues of racial discrimination, faith, and finding one's own voice. Along the way in facing difficulty and in the telling of my own story, I am reminded of what the Lord says to us: "Do not be afraid or discouraged because of this vast army. For the battle is not yours, but the Lord's" (2 Chr 20:15 NIV). The word of God in Hebrews 12:3 boldly asserts to all (segregationists and non-segregationists) who dare to follow Christ: "Consider Him who has endured such hostility by sinners against Himself, so that you may not grow weary and lose heart." But for one student seeking attention by becoming the "class clown," it is easy for an African American sixth grader to "grow weary."

This is where my own story begins. In the community of my childhood, my close posse of friends called me "Bud." "Bud . . . you had better stop goofing off so much in my class and playing around with your friends . . . if you keep up this track record, you'll surely throw away your future . . . I think I just may have to have a talk with your parents." I vividly remember these stern words of discipline that fell from the lips of Mrs. Martin before the whole class. Naturally, at that moment, I felt extremely embarrassed and ashamed. Rhetorically, we may ask the question: Who is Mrs. Martin? Well, since you may be curious about the unfolding drama, allow me to introduce you to an extraordinary woman. As a public school educator, Mrs. Martin was my sixth-grade Social Studies teacher. However, her particular area of academic interest or expertise was American history. She was a popular person on the faculty of Dunbar High School (Earle, Arkansas), and well respected and admired by both colleagues and students.

In retrospect, Mrs. Martin's stern advice to me—though it didn't feel good at the moment—was justified. Now the ragged details of the particular incident in Mrs. Martin's class actually involved my *casual attitude* about doing her homework assignments properly. On two or three of the standard assignments, I recall receiving "D" or low "C" grades. She knew me well as a student—this was out of character with my academic performance at previous grade levels in elementary school. By the way, Mrs. Martin was also a devout Christian and taught a youth Bible class at St. James Missionary Baptist Church. As a matter of fact, she lived a few houses down from the church. However, my greatest anxiety or fear, existentially, was that Mrs. Martin would consult my parents about my goofing-off behavior in her class. For better or worse, in the neighborhood where I grew up, nothing significant that happened at Dunbar High School got past your parents. Metaphorically, it seemed as if the neighborhood had a thousands eyes and a thousand ears. Put another way, the *word* in the neighborhood always got back to your parents regarding one's academic performance in school. It is only a glimpse into the obvious to suggest that elders in the community *deeply cared* about the well being of each child. Although many parents in the down-home culture of Earle had only a seventh or eighth-grade education, they wanted more for their children. Teachers—like parents—knew that education meant a way out of poverty.

Education was the key that unlocked the future for our children. Reflectively, I can remember that Mrs. Martin perceived it, as did many teachers in the neighborhood, as the great equalizer between black and white people in southern society. In short, I knew that Mrs. Martin would report to my parents about my goofing-off behavior in her sixth-grade class. Thus, she reported to my parents. I felt ashamed and embarrassed. I desired to do something about it. As a gifted educator, Mrs. Martin believed in the potential and self-directed faith of each child to succeed in life. "No exceptions . . . no lame excuses," she would often mutter to the class. Though I did not fully realize it at the time, our teachers and community elders deeply cared about our wellbeing and safety—as they lifted their courageous voices against the educational status quo in the late 1950s and early 1960s. In the language of Marian Wright Edelman in her acclaimed book *Lanterns*, "they (i.e., teachers and parents) expected us to achieve and we did."

However, my own moments of self-awareness and spiritual awakening came for me as I transitioned from the sixth to the seventh grade. I suddenly realized that I must take personal responsibility for my own learning and education. I realized that Mrs. Martin could lead me to the fountain of knowledge and a *new perspective* on our world, but she couldn't make me drink. She could *instruct* by way of a lesson plan in the classroom, but my own young mind had to be open and willing to think through critical moral issues in society. One such issue, of which I had to struggle, was the issue of self-reliance. By this I mean trying to take responsibility for one's own actions and being in the world that's not easy. Why? It forces us to look deep inside ourselves. Perhaps the filmmaker Spike Lee had it right when he once said to a crowd of students at Morehouse College (Atlanta, Georgia), these poignant words: "we can't rely on anyone but ourselves to define our existence, to shape the image of ourselves."

I suspect that learning to take responsibility for one's education is very difficult in a culture where goofing off in class was often rewarded with praises from one's friends. In Mrs. Martin I found, while thinking about the far-reaching world of goofing off, that such behavior did not make me feel better inside. Indeed, I believe there is no more serious or important time in a young person's life than when he *comes to himself*, when he finally comes home to the compassionate arms of care (Luke 15:11–32). In a strange sense, I was that prodigal son—goofing off before my friends and desperately trying to play the role of the class clown in the sixth grade. Hence, such a pattern of behavior needed to be under the thumb of self-discipline and a new orientation in regard to the pursuit of education. Therefore, it is not a stretch of the imagination to affirm that true "education is the jewel," says Mari Evans, "casting brilliance into the future." Looking back, Mrs. Martin helped me to see the "God-piece" and the "decency-piece" buried inside me; and more importantly, I didn't have to be the class clown in order to win friends and to find acceptance from others.

Ultimately, I suspect that there is no sure way of gauging the distinguished lifetime legacy of Rosa Parks, except to say that she left the world a much better place in which we *all* can live. In retrospect, the Montgomery Bus Boycott lasted 382 days and brought Mrs. Parks, Dr. King, and their cause to the attention of the world community. A Supreme Court decision struck down the Montgomery ordinance under which Mrs. Parks had been fined and outlawed racial segregation on public transportation. To this day, The Southern Christian Leadership Council holds an annual Rosa Parks Freedom Award celebration in her honor.

Mrs. Parks, along with the support of the Institute, sponsored an annual summer program for teenagers called Pathways to Freedom. To this day, young people tour the country in buses, under adult supervision, learning the history of their country and of the Civil Rights movement. President Clinton presented Rosa Parks with the Presidential Medal of Freedom in 1996. She received a Congressional Gold Medal in 1999.

When asked about the future and the divisive forces of ethnic hatred in the world, she replied with optimism: "There is only one world . . . and yet, we as a people, have treated the world as if it were divided. We cannot allow the gains we have made to erode."[27]

Mrs. Parks spent her last years living quietly in Detroit, where she died in 2005 at the age of 92. After her death, her casket was placed in the rotunda of the United States Capitol for two days so the nation could pay its respects to the woman whose courage had changed the lives of so many. She was the first woman in American history to lie in state at the Capitol, an honor usually reserved for Presidents of the United States.

Coretta Scott King's Early Years: Some Hard Days

Countless historians and theologians over the last four decades have carefully documented the outstanding contributions of Martin Luther King, Jr. to civil and human rights. In the throes of urban life in nearly every American city, there are streets, monuments, and schools that proudly wear the famous name: Martin Luther King, Jr. For many ordinary American citizens, the idea of seeing "Martin" as an icon of our post-modern culture is common knowledge. Perhaps some will remember, in his classic book *Stride Toward Freedom*, how Martin gave the global community a prophetic word when he muttered: "the guiding principle is . . . non-violent resistance . . . Today the choice is no longer between violence and non-violence. The choice is either non-violence or non-existence."[28] Of course, many interesting volumes have been written, either in public life or in the religious life of the community, on the critical thought of "Martin," who inevitably earned a PhD degree in Systematic Theology from Boston University. *But who in the world was Coretta?* Well, it is prudent and graceful to note that on their wedding day of June 18, 1953, Coretta made it known before the world that she was not going to be just another "traditional housewife," fulfilling society's prescribed parental roles, expectations, and duties assigned to women based on the myth of feminist inferiority. Rather she articulated the view that her marriage would resemble more of an "equal partnership of love," as they embraced a common vision beyond themselves. Indeed, Coretta Scott was driven by what I call a "womanist spirit," as she enrolled in the New England Conservatory of Music in Boston with the expressed purpose of following in the esteemed footsteps of Marian Anderson. As a concert artist, the color bar at the Metropolitan Opera Company, for example, was not lowered until January 7, 1955, when Marian Anderson appeared as Ulrica in Verdi's "*Un Ballo in Maschera.*" The artist Arturo Toscanini heard her melodious voice in 1935 and proclaimed: "A voice like yours is heard only once in a hundred years."[29] So then, Coretta was a young progressive woman possessing a career purpose even before meeting Martin. After their marriage, she never really conformed to the traditional image of a pastor's wife at Dexter Avenue Baptist Church in Montgomery. She was a modern-day womanist in the full sense of the term. *Courage, faith,* and *elegance* are the three cardinal words that best depict the engaging boundaries of the personality of Coretta Scott King.

Existentially speaking, I first met Mrs. Coretta Scott King during the 1970s as a PhD doctoral student in social ethics at Boston University while doing collaborative research on Martin Luther King, Jr., as a "new paradigm" in black theology. She was the keynote speaker for an evening banquet among students campus wide. Later in my teaching career as an ethical theologian, I would often see this peace-loving activist and civil rights leader stroll pass my office en route to work at her own office, as we shared common space in the central administration building of the Interdenominational Theological Center (I.T.C.), Atlanta, Georgia in the mid–1970s. At the time, I served full-time on the faculty of the I.T.C. as the Andrew W. Mellon Assistant Professor of Christian Ethics and Chairman of Church and Society. It is only a glimpse into the obvious to suggest that the current institution, the Martin Luther King, Jr., Center for Non-Violent Social Change, had not yet been completed. Therefore, we were sharing a common floor (lower level) for office work, in the main building of the I.T.C. Those were fun days of mutual dialogue, occasional fellowship, and deep respect for a legacy I had come to love: *the mutual legacy of Coretta and Martin Luther King, Jr.*

As a womanist thinker, I strongly believe and affirm that the cardinal virtue of "courage" seems to mark the outward garment of her personality. "One is not necessarily born with courage," says Maya Angelou, "but one is born with potential. Without courage, we cannot practice any other virtue with consistency."[30]

As heaven's blessing gently showed favor upon the earth, Coretta Scott King was born in Heiberger, Alabama on April 27, 1927, the third of four children to Bernice McMurray and Obadiah "Obie" Scott. She inherited, undoubtedly, a rich legacy of leadership, family values, faith, and a respect for the ethic of work as a tool for economic empowerment and educational advancement in our society. She was named for her grandmother, Cora, a woman of unusual strength and drive. Although Coretta never knew her grandmother, she was often told that she was much like her.[31]

Her father, maternal grandmother, and slave-born maternal grandfather all grew up and sold produce in the community. Coretta's mother and maternal grandmother were—like Rosa Parks—seamstresses. So then, one of Coretta's deepest regrets was never having known her grandma Cora.[32]

Perhaps a surprise to none in the Civil Rights movement, the whole Scott family believed that work is *honorable* whether that work be chicken farming, the lumber industry, or the cotton industry. They practiced—seemingly unrepentantly—the Protestant work ethic of frugality, prudence, and the value of laying aside savings for a better future. The noted black educator Booker T. Washington, for instance, equated work with the nobility of building up civilization and the economy. As a businessman, Coretta's father was so successful in combining the art of chicken farming and lumber hauling, until he was regarded as the first "colored man" in the county to actually own his own sawmill. In 1946, he opened a grocery on his own property. As a result of these and other entrepreneurial activities, white men often threatened him and the security of the Scott family. Mrs. Scott instilled into the consciousness of young Coretta the religio-cultural values of truth, honesty, compassion, faith, and a love for freedom.

As an introduction to these pivotal values, young Coretta knew, almost instinctively, that the ethic of work must figure into the moral equation. When Coretta entered school, she joined other community children in walking over four miles to Crossroads School.[33] This is not unlike many other black children of that generation, who embraced the ethic of social struggle and work. Thanks be to God that many of us have come to see that work means more than just a job. Work means more than a mere paycheck—although these are important economic indicators. Work also means human dignity. For example, I recall the prophetic and firm words of Martin Luther King, Jr., during his tragic visit to Memphis to help garbage workers. There he emphatically proclaimed:

> We are demanding that this city (Memphis) respect the dignity of labor. So often we overlook the work and the significance of those who are not in professional jobs, of those who are not in the so-called big jobs. Let me say to you (sanitation workers) whenever you are engaged in work that serves humanity and is for the building up of humanity, it has dignity, it has worth.[34]

Of course, no morally sensitive person can deny the value inherent in the dignity of work. After completing the sixth grade at Crossroads, young Coretta joined her sister at Lincoln High School in Marion, Alabama. The Scott family placed a high value on education. Accordingly, the Scott's paid $4.50 in tuition for each child as well as room and board for their children to live with a family during the week. White children were bused to Marion High School daily. But in young Coretta's junior year, the county allotted some funds for transportation for black students; and Mr. Scott had the creativity to convert an old truck into a bus that Mrs. Scott drove a total of 40 miles each day.

In the world of social struggle, enormous sacrifices were made on the part of the parents of young Coretta, her older sister, Edythe, and brother, Obie Leonard, to receive the best possible education. In the drama of her formal educational narrative, the womanist spirit of Coretta Scott suggests to us that is why she graduated as valedictorian of her class at Lincoln High School in 1945. What a majestic intellectual achievement, which challenges us all to remember the biblical text: "Study to show your self approved unto God, a workman that need not be ashamed but rightly divides the word of truth" (2 Tim 2:15). In 1951, this promising young leader graduated from Antioch College with a Bachelor of Arts Degree in Elementary Education and Music. However, in 1954, Coretta Scott King had already hooked her wagon to a "star" after receiving a Bachelor of Music Degree in Education with a major in voice and a minor in violin from the New England Conservatory of Music. Of course, in 1955, the King's first child, daughter Yolanda Denise, was born on November 17, and, as the saying goes, *"the rest is the history of a noble American family."* In the throes of history and work itself, Coretta Scott King also knew something about cotton picking.

The spirit of womanist ethics does not mean that Coretta Scott King did not know something of the history and economic impact of the cotton industry upon southern blacks and the wider society. As I have already pointed out, words like "womanism" and "womanist" did not appear in the regular patterns of Afrocentric speech in the mid–1950s and 1960s by women such as Rosa Parks, Coretta Scott King, or Dr. Dorothy Height—especially as a way of describing the interests, affairs, and unique experiences of women. However, words like "cotton sacks," "cotton fields," or "cotton gins" were commonplace expressions in the popular grassroots culture of the black community in the South during the 1940s and 1950s—two hard decades of racial segregation in America. It has been said, of course, that young Coretta, picked cotton herself.

Coretta began working for a white cotton farmer at the age of ten. She dug long rows, making sure the width of a hoe was between each stalk. When the puffs were ready, she worked as a cotton picker, making from $4 to $5 dollars a season. She once picked 200 pounds of cotton a day earning an astonishing $7 dollars. She learned in the cotton fields not only to endure tough situations, but also to overcome them. She was known to consistently pick more cotton than her male cousins.[35] I can identify with that same reality as Coretta Scott King, because I, too, picked cotton—growing up as an African American youth in the state of Arkansas.

On the practical level, in the culture of cotton, I remember how young black youths—including my friends and myself—learned the art of work, discipline, social responsibility and contributing to the family's budget. By the same token, I suspect that words like "grace," "strength," "character," "courage," and "faith" were the sort of moral *stuff* that best describe the formative years of young Coretta as she grew up in Perry County, Alabama, knowing something about the culture of cotton. Indeed, the tealeaves of American history suggest that in the 1940s and 1950s, there was a phenomenon known as "cotton patch religion" in the South. Accordingly, the moral agent may logically ask: "what, then, is cotton patch religion in the context of Coretta Scott King's story?" Well, I suspect that the language of cotton patch religion is a language of struggle, hope, and freedom from all forms of oppression. For Christian believers, biblical faith makes a powerful point for all of us to remember, namely: "for freedom Christ has set us free, do not re-submit to the yoke of bondage" (Gal 5:1). Moreover, the language of cotton patch religion declares that, segregation may knock you down but it can't keep you down. The language of cotton patch religion affirms that Christians or true believers may have to go through the *pain* of a humiliating condition; but beyond the pain, God restores the passion to continue onward and upward toward one's destiny. God wants to raise each of us to a higher level. Undoubtedly, the song that I remember which best illustrates the resilience of cotton patch religion was regularly sung at worship on Sunday morning by our gospel choir at St. James Missionary Baptist Church, in Earle. The song title, *"Lord Plant my Feet on Higher Ground,"* and its refrain went like this:

> Lord, lift me up and let me stand;
> My faith on Heaven's Table land,
> A higher place than I have found,
> Lord plant my feet on higher ground.
> Lord, Lift me up!
> Lord, Lift me up!
> Lord, Lift me up!

As a follower of Christ and ambassador of peace and justice, Coretta Scott King found strength in one of her favorite songs, *"This Little Light*

of Mine, I'm Goin' t' Let It Shine." Strength for the journey is what we all
need. Every lover of justice just needs a *little* light, any bit of light that
can penetrate the darkness of racial bigotry and hatred. Coretta, therefore,
would never let go of the power of a little light, which provided the gift of
shining amidst the sinfulness and darkness of this present age. The song-
writer or poet echoes:

> This little light of mine, I'm goin' t' let it shine,
> This little light of mine, I'm goin' t' let it shine,
> This little light of mine, I'm goin' t' let it shine,
> Let it shine, let it shine, let it shine.
> All through the night, I'm goin' to let it shine, . . .
> Everywhere I go, I'm goin' to let it shine, . . .
> Let it shine, let it shine, let it shine.[36]

The language of cotton patch religion brings *light* and radiance that
can shine upon our paths in life. Why not expose one's light and not keep
it under a bushel (Matt 5:14–15). The genius inherent in the language of
cotton patch religion arises, not from the fact that humans fall down, but
humans get up again: i.e., getting up from the ditches of depression; getting up from the ditches of anxiety and fear; getting up from the ditches
of conformity and loyalty of other people's expectations *for us*; getting
up from the ditches of drugs, drifting, and excessive drinking; getting up
from the ditches of crass materialism and living *above* our means as status
"symbols" of success; and above all, getting up from ditches of an uncritical desire to please others rather than to be pleasing in the sight of God
(Prov 16:7; Isa 55:11; Heb 11:5). A brief historical note seems appropriate
at this point in regard to the vitality of cotton in the southern region of
the United States.

It is important for us to remember that in 1792 Eli Whitney in-
vented the famous cotton gin. This event changed the base of the southern
economy. The centerpiece of this "new economy" was slave labor. Cotton
quickly became the major southern crop. Now in order to grow enough
cotton to meet the demand and to keep the cotton gins running, large
numbers of workers or "pickers" were needed. Hence, the growth of "King
Cotton" resulted in the expansion of slavery, and the economic prosperity
of southern whites—based largely on black labor, exploitation, and the
demoralization of people from African descent. Slaves were treated like
cattle, as if they were insensitive to pain, hurt, hunger, thirst, cold, fear,
or loneliness. Looking back, as a child of the South, blacks were survivors
of slavery, thanks be to God. Indeed, during the most dreadful days of

African bondage in America, enslaved blacks did much more than pick cotton. Like my father only three decades removed from legalized slavery in the U.S.A., some blacks were carpenters and barbers. Some were blacksmiths and painters. Some were seamstresses and scientists. Some were inventors and novelists. Some were preachers and revolutionaries. The bottom line of this historic snapshot seems to suggest that there were so many highly skilled black men and women that even job opportunities for white immigrants were, perhaps, limited.

So then, briefly considered, I suspect that the courage, character, and work-ethic of Coretta Scott King was shaped, in part, by the culture of cotton which was so persistent and common to the wider ethos of southern society.

Partnership in the Struggle

Profoundly spiritual and self-energizing, Coretta and Martin worked as *partners* in the struggle for freedom, justice, and equality for all of God's Children: Black and White, Asians and Latinos, Native Americans and poor European Americans, and all the hurting ones in our global community. The term "partnership" implies two or more people working together to realize a common purpose or dream. It implies "joint interest"; it means two persons dancing to the beat of the same drummer. I suspect that wherever any reasonable individual in our global community finds oneself, the echoing testimony would likely be the same: *Coretta and Martin were both drum majors for justice and peace all over the world.*

As a womanist voice for justice and peace, I strongly believe that God ordained Coretta to be in *partnership* with Martin in the *struggle* that the moral forces of history had authorized. "And so our struggle continues as still we rise," says Myrlie Evers-Williams, "to beat back the snarling dogs of segregation."[37] For both Coretta and Martin, struggle appears to be a test of character and will. Struggle is not a transcendent reality; but rather it is a reality that empowers us to transcend whatever trial or difficulty in life. Advocates of the Civil Rights movement knew that there is a sense of social solidarity in struggle. There is sense of common identity in struggle. There is song and dance in struggle. There is joy in struggle. There is power in struggle. There is the possibility of authentic freedom in the whirlwinds of struggle itself. For Coretta and Martin, the notion of *partnership in the struggle* was, therefore, symbolic of the entire Civil Rights Freedom Movement in the mid-1950s and 1960s. Through one's spiritual eyes of faith, it was as if Coretta and Martin spoke to us in "protest parables" and dared us not to forget the meaning of collective struggle. While facing difficult days and, often, sleepless nights in our society today, their moral and spiritual legacy say to the world and particular members of the Christian community. Here I offer this personal poetic musing, in light of their vision for the church and lovers of freedom and democracy around the world:

> Look for us in the whirlwind or storm of racial segregation in America; look around for us in rat infested jails . . . fighting for the good cause of freedom . . . my own letter from the 'Birmingham Jail' was not written to "*white clergymen*," for countless millions of ex-black slaves only . . . but for the salvation and soul of America's freedom and democracy . . .

> As you move about this day, look around for us in the laughter of children as they play; and do not notice skin color: Red, Yellow, Black, or White. Children only know . . . they are precious in God's sight.

> As you move about this day, look around for us in every courthouse that loves justice; and every church house that loves Jesus! Ultimately, look for us, as you journey through life, not in the whirlwind of bigotry's grit; but in the bosom of God's grace.

The ethical bottom line is simple as it is awesome: Coretta Scott King and Martin Luther King, Jr. had a rare covenant of love that demonstrated to us, and before the whole world the value of a *partnership in the struggle*. To be sure, at every critical point in the Freedom Movement, the womanist genius of Coretta Scott King was present.

In 1964, she accompanied Dr. King to Oslo, Norway, where he received the Nobel Peace Prize. Even prior to her husband's first public statement against the Vietnam War in 1967, Mrs. King functioned as liaison to peace and justice organizations and as an advocate for the unheard and disadvantaged in the councils of public officials.[38]

After her husband's assassination in 1968, instead of retreating with her young children into grief, Coretta Scott King stepped out into the forefront to continue her husband's legacy. She began this the day before his funeral, leading the sanitation workers' march he had gone to Memphis to support. She continued to stand up for social justice for the rest of her life. Mrs. King was devoted to preserving Dr. King's legacy by committing much of her energy and attention to developing and building the Atlanta-based Martin Luther King, Jr. Center for Nonviolent Social Change as a living memorial to her husband's life and nonviolent philosophy.[39]

Situated in the Freedom Hall Complex encircling Dr. King's tomb, the King Center is part of a twenty-three acre national historic park which includes his birth home and which hosts more than one million visitors a year. For the twenty-seven years between 1968 and 1995, Mrs. King devoted her life to developing the King Center, the first institution built in honor of an African American leader. As the Founding President, Chair, and Chief Operating Executive Officer, she dedicated herself to providing local, national and international programs that have trained tens of thousands of people in Dr. King's nonviolence philosophy and methods. She guided the creation of the largest archives in the world of Civil Rights documents at the King Center. In 1995, she passed the torch of leadership to her son Dexter Scott King. Also, Bernice, her daughter, followed the path of Christian ministry as her father had done decades earlier.[40]

Mrs. King spearheaded the massive educational and lobbying campaign to establish Dr. King's birthday as a national holiday. In 1984, at the request of Mrs. King, Congress established the Martin Luther King, Jr. Federal Holiday Commission to assure appropriate commemoration of Dr. King's birthday throughout the nation and world. Mrs. King was the commission's Chair for its duration. On the third Monday in January 1986, the first official national holiday in honor of Dr. King was celebrated. The King holiday is now celebrated by all 50 states and by millions of people in more than 100 countries.[41]

Coretta Scott King has carried the message of nonviolence and the dream of the "beloved community" throughout the world. As a theologian and prophetic leader, Dr. King spoke passionately about the concept of the beloved community. For King, it is radically connected with love, reconciliation, and the salvation of civilization as we have come to know it. He wrote: "Love may well be the salvation of our civilization . . . . It is true that as we struggle for freedom in America, we will have to boycott at times. But we must remember . . . that a boycott is not an end in itself . . . . But the end is reconciliation; the end is redemption; the end is the creation of the beloved community. It is this type of spirit and this type of love that can transform opponents into friends. It is this type of understanding goodwill that will transform the deep gloom of the old age into the exuberant gladness of the new age."[42]

As a partner in struggle, Coretta's womanist instinct did not lead to moral insomnia, but rather a bold recognition that the essence of the moral life in the beloved community is primarily informed by love—a type of love that liberates and reconciles. There is a peculiar manner, in one's reflections upon race relations in America, in which King spoke of liberation (i.e., authentic freedom), reconciliation, and the love-ethic as a phenomenon intricately related to the concept of the beloved community.[43]

Here we may discern that Dr. King's conception of the beloved community is the vision of the "new age"—the age of liberation for all oppressed people.[44] Ethically, the so-called "new age" is a social vision of the new society; one in which racial hatred is rejected and communal love is radically affirmed for all the saints of God. Both Coretta and Martin strongly believed and held the moral conviction that it is only by projecting the power of love to the center of our lives that we will be able to "cut loose the chains of racial hatred," and follow a more excellent way as dramatized in the life of Jesus. Seemingly, both Coretta and Martin knew deep within their souls a certain wellspring of poetry inherent in the oral tradition of the black church, which helped to nurture the concept of the beloved community by echoing this vision about Jesus as seen through my own mind's eye:

> To the oppressed-millions in the Land, Jesus is Liberator
> To the segregationist, he is Savior, if you repent.
> To the hungry, Jesus is food on the table.
> To the thirsty, he is the gushing fountain that never runs dry.
> To the sick he is the Wounded Healer and a Balm in Gilead.
> To the womanist theologian he is manifested wisdom and
> Compassionate Knowledge of who God is;
> To the philosopher he is the moral insight guiding our tedious pathway.
> To the geologist he is the Rock of Ages.
> To the lawyer he is the Counselor, the Lawgiver who advocates
> for Justice and Peace.
> To the stranger, he is the Friend who stays closer than a sister or brother.
> To the womanist spirit, Jesus is the "Breaker" of Jewish tradition
> By equally honoring the gifts of women.
> To the poor he is Divine favor and the Abundant life.
> To the one who suffers from low self-esteem, Jesus says:
> "I love you . . . you are somebody, you are a child of God!"

In her classic book, *My Life With Martin Luther King, Jr.*, Coretta describes the force of a mutual partnership in which she inevitably affirmed: "I did not marry a man *only*, but a vision." Like the dynamic fabric of the Civil Rights movement itself, Coretta Scott King symbolized for us, as ethically concerned persons of the twenty-first century, a pivotal unifying thread by the force of her own character and self-determination to keep alive the "Dream." It is only a glimpse into the obvious to suggest that

Coretta Scott King—a womanist thinker, with a "sassy" freedom-loving spirit—was the primary *Keeper of the Dream*.

Ethically, the core of the Dream for both Coretta and Martin was the creation of a world community free from the wretchedness of violence, war, injustice, and racial discrimination. As partners in the struggle, they both believed that the politics of violence, at any time and for whatever reason, is morally and ethically wrong. As partners in the struggle, they both believed not in a "color-blind" America, but in a united America where all people respect the positive gifts of ethnicity and cultural diversity. As partners in the struggle, they strongly advocated that the walls of separation brought on by legal and *de facto* segregation, and discrimination based on race, must be eradicated—in light of the biblical principles of Christian faith and the moral tenets undergirding the U.S. Constitution. As partners in the struggle, Coretta and Martin spoke to us not only about the critical issues of poverty, racism, and war; but they also made plain to us a philosophy of nonviolence as a *way of life*, not simply as a strategy to achieve social change. Accordingly, Coretta tells the story of a mass meeting one night, when Martin reflected on his own fate and the importance of "staying the course" of nonviolence. He thundered to the crowd:

> If one day you find me sprawled and dead, I do not want you to retaliate with a single act of violence. I urge you to continue protesting with the same dignity and discipline you have shown so far.[45]

The King family constantly tendered "threats" of death, abusive calls, bombing, and angry voices to his home that muttered in the night: "Listen, Nigger . . . stop this Civil Rights movement now or else." This kind of stress and abuse made Coretta and Martin feel very weary. Apparently, one day Martin just couldn't take anymore, so he approached God in prayer saying, "Lord, I am taking a stand for what I believe is right. The people are looking to me for leadership, and if I stand before them without strength and courage, they will falter. I am at the end of my powers. I have nothing left. I've come to the point where I can't fact it alone."[46] Now after this desperate cry unto the Lord for help, Coretta remembered Martin also saying to her:

> At that moment I experienced the presence of the Divine as I had never experienced Him before. It seemed as though I could hear the quiet assurance of an inner voice saying: 'Stand up for righteousness; stand up for truth, and God will be at your side forever.'[47]

As a woman of faith, Coretta recalled that in the radical certainty of the moment, Martin's experience with the Divine empowered him—despite racial protest and hot summers of discontent—to face anything that Jim Crowism threw his way. As life-giving partners in the struggle for authentic freedom, justice and peace, both Coretta and Martin leave behind a rich legacy of courage and strength. Joshua 1:9 says: "Be strong and of a good courage, be not afraid, neither be though dismayed: for the Lord thy God is with thee whithersoever thou goest." As a womanist voice dedicated to the fulfillment of his dream, Coretta Scott King never caved in to a self-defeating attitude, an unfair criticism of the movement or the politics of deception and possessive individualism in American culture. But rather as a "diamond in formation," expressive of a tough mind and tender heart, Coretta seemed to have always taken the moral high ground in regard to the critical issues at stake in both church and society. In a recent article by Ambassador Andrew Young entitled, "*The Untold Story of Martin Luther King, Jr. and Coretta Scott King*," the following complimentary words were muttered by the Ambassador: "Coretta Scott King seemed to toughen in the difficulties of her life from childhood, through the movement, in her loneliness . . . She became 'diamond-like' in her character. The more savage the criticism, the gossip and controversy, the more she seemed to shine. Her beauty and countenance never wavered."[48]

To be sure, the prophetic voices of Rosa Parks, Coretta Scott King, and Martin Luther King, Jr. are no longer in our midst *physically*. Yet it is my moral conviction that their *dream* lives on in the hearts of countless millions of people around the world, who dare to love freedom, justice, and peace as the benchmarks of human dignity and community.

While they are not physically with us, their legacy and vision must live on inside of us like a tree planted by the rivers of water that brings forth fruit in its season—"bearing fruit with the seed in it. And God saw that it was good" (Gen 1:12; Rev 22:2). As icons to remember and to be internalized in our own value system, the leaves from their "trees" were good for the healing of the nation. Simple as it is awesome, their legacy and vision live inside of us as a roadmap to the future.

Women, men, youth, and children who make up the amazingly powerful story of American democracy as well as the learned and marginalized people around the world are all heirs of the *Dream*. Our nation is made better because of the *Dream*. Womanist ethics and black theology find "new life" in the rhythmic flux of creativity and the breakthrough of spiritual boundaries because of the dream. Indeed, I suspect that the black church in contemporary society must be the *constant guardian* of the dream, if African Americans and other people of color are to be fully loosed from the perennial chains of sexism, racism, and violence that so easily afflict our nation and world. As partners in the struggle—Red, Yellow, Black or White—we as the people of God are, ultimately, bound by a covenantal imperative, namely: *to report for duty on a daily basis as faithful keepers of the Dream.* In the final analysis, reflecting back on the long difficult struggle for freedom, Martin said this about Coretta's inner strength and character:

> I am convinced that if I had not had a wife with the fortitude, strength and calmness of Coretta, I could not have stood up amid the ordeals and tensions surrounding the Montgomery movement. I came to see the real meaning of that rather trite statement: "A wife can either make or break a husband." Coretta proved to be that type of wife with qualities to make a husband when he could have been so easily broken. In the darkest moments she always brought the light of hope.[49]

Teaser Test
The Civil Rights Movement
(Answer Sheet follows Case Study)

Multiple Choice:

1. Dr. King was born in what city?
   a. Birmingham, Alabama   c. Atlanta, Georgia
   b. Montgomery, Alabama   d. Macon, George

2. Dr. King was born on what date?
   a. January 25, 1928   c. January 15, 1930
   b. January 4, 1928   d. January 15, 1929

3. Which institution did *not* play a role in Dr. King's higher education?
   a. Colgate Rochester Seminary   c. Morehouse College
   b. Crozer Theological Seminary   d. Boston University Seminary

4. Rosa Parks refused to give up her seat on the bus because she was . . .
   a. tired from her work day   c. tired of changing seats
   b. tired of the system of segregation   d. tired of sitting beside strangers

5. The Montgomery Bus Boycott lasted how long?
   a. Approximately two years   c. Approximately three weeks
   b. From December into January   d. Approximately one year

6. Which mode of transportation was *not* a part of the bus boycott?
   a. Walking   c. Bicycles
   b. Rapid Transit System   d. Mules/wagons

7. Dr. King, Jr. was co-pastor with his father at what church?
   a. St. Paul Baptist Church   c. Dexter Ave. Baptist Church
   b. Ebenezer Baptist Church   d. Antioch Baptist Church

True-False Questions:

_____Ralph David Abernathy was one of Dr. King's strong opponents in the Civil Rights movement.

_____Martin met his future wife, Coretta, while he was a developing student at Crozer Theological Seminary.

_____Dr. King wrote his PhD dissertation on the critical thought of Reinhold Niebuhr.

_____Martin King understood the philosophy of non-violence as both a strategy for social change and a way of life.

_____In the early 1960s, Martin Luther King, Jr. wrote the popular book *The Next Time*.

_____Dr. King wrote the book, *Why We Can't Wait*.

_____In 1957, Dr. King became the pastor of Antioch Baptist Church in Montgomery, Alabama.

_____Martin and Coretta were the proud parents of four children, namely: Yolanda, Bernice, Dexter, and Martin, III.

_____The "*I Have a Dream*" speech was delivered on August 24, 1964 in Washington, D.C.

_____On March 2, 1955, Claudette Colvin, a 15-year-old high school student, refused a bus driver's demand to give up her seat to whites.

_____Mrs. Jo Ann Robinson, President of the Women's Political Council (WPC), was a key community activist in the Montgomery Bus Boycott movement.

Completion:

Write one or two major events that took place in these cities during the Civil Rights movement.

1. Montgomery, Alabama

2. Greensboro, North Carolina

3. Selma, Alabama

4. Birmingham, Alabama

5. Washington, D. C.

6. Oslo, Norway

7. Memphis, Tennessee

Case Study: Black Women in the Pew, Black Men in the Pulpit.

"I must confess as a Christian and member of this committee . . . that I feel uneasy and uncomfortable with the hasty decision . . . and rush to judgment on our part to elect another male candidate . . . for pastoral leadership in our church family . . . without seriously considering a qualified woman called by God to ministry . . . this feels ethically wrong to me. . . . . Without doubt, I have faith in our work, but I'm gonna let go of my duties on this committee."

These are the words that fell from the lips of Sally Harris, a 36-year-old single parent and mother of two lovely children, Rebecca, 5, and little Eric, 3 years old. Sally comes from a middle class family background, with deep religio-cultural roots in the black community of Cleveland, Ohio. Her mother, Lois Harris, was a dedicated public school teacher, specializing in Early Childhood Development; and her father, Henry Harris, has a successful practice as a dentist. Educationally speaking, Sally grew up in a nurturing home environment as she readily embraced values of faith, hard work, and a willing spirit to do well in life. Accordingly, her parents sent her to Spelman College in Atlanta where she earned a Bachelor of Arts Degree in Public Communications. As a young urban professional, she stayed on in the city of Atlanta and was fortunate to carve out a job for herself in the pubic media industry.

From a historical viewpoint, Sally's parents as well as grandparents have been members of the Corner Stone Baptist Church of Cleveland for many generations. As a matter of fact, Sally can never remember when she was not a part of the nurturing love, hospitality, and religious instruction of the Christian church. As an African American youth, she "literally blossomed," morally and spiritually, as a child of the Corner Stone Church family. So then, after a successful career in Atlanta, Sally returns to her hometown church and ends up on the official search committee for a new pastor.

To the inquiring mind, Corner Stone itself has a unique history. "Convinced of the saving Love of Jesus," a small group of slaves escaped from the Deep South and migrated to Cleveland where they established the church in 1856. This was the time when most Southern blacks were illiterate, but there was one book they did know something about—orally and figuratively—and that was the Bible, the living word of God. Thus Corner Stone first opened its doors for Christian worship seven years prior to the final *Emancipation Proclamation* on January 1, 1863, at which point

Lincoln declared that slaves in areas still in rebellion "shall be then, henceforward, and forever free!"

But the matter under consideration in this case is not our musings over the unique history of the Corner Stone Church family in regard to the antebellum slave experience of "shouting," "praying" and "testifying," about the goodness of God. It is not even about the fact that, in its rich history, only men have occupied the pastoral office. Rather Sally's discontentment and rebellion, as a member of the pastoral search process, arises from a crisis of conscience with six other persons on the committee.

Apparently, Sally stormed out of the committee in anger and protest because the process did not leave room for a serious look at a woman minister as full-time pastor. Joyce Jackson, another member of the search committee, expressed doubts and fear as she muttered in a heated discussion: "We've never had a woman as lead pastor over our church . . . I don't think people in the pews are ready for . . . . Besides, I'm afraid that our present membership of 375 may plummet . . . if we had a woman in the pulpit preaching every Sunday morning."

Sally's response to Joyce was something less than favorable. She cracked: "Joyce, that kind of attitude belongs to the dark ages of ministry. We live in a new day and must try out new possibilities of pastoral leadership . . . if we want to give our young daughters a different role model in the life of the local church." After a rather agonizing conversation with Joyce, other members remained virtually silent as Sally left the meeting feeling that her concerns about moral issues had not been addressed. For Sally, this was a "justice" issue—just like racism is a justice issue—because the committee had not seriously considered a woman for pastor, although over half of the people who faithfully attend Sunday morning worship and praise service are women. In a quiet moment of reflection, Sally Harris gently reminded a few trusted people on the pastoral search committee of a perennial irony: *African American Christian women fill most of the pews at Corner Stone Baptist Church, while the pulpit is usually dominated by men.*

She is then left to ponder, deep within her own spirit and soul these questions: What's going on with God's people, in light of women called to ministry in the black church tradition? Like the growing pains of life, does God care? In the lived world of experience, what is the most loving thing to do in deciding between a man or woman equally qualified to assume pastoral leadership?

These were the sorts of moral questions and concerns that turned over in Sally's mind as she agonized over leaving the search committee behind. As a Christian however, Sally neither wavered from her strong faith in God, nor did she ever leave her Corner Stone Church family behind. Inevitably, Sally Harris strongly believed that the *justice* of her position would ultimately, be vindicated by God. Galatians 6:9 says, "Let us not grow weary while doing good, for in due season we shall reap if we do not lose heart."

Ethical Approach

1. Try looking at this case from the viewpoint of your own experiences and values growing up as a girl or boy?

2. Confronting the power of *sexism* in the church, how would you likely advise the ones on the pastoral search committee who differed with Sally's ethical stance?

3. Is there a link between the forces of racism and sexism as you look at the stories and contributions of Rosa Parks and Coretta Scott King in our society today?

4. How can a womanist ethic of compassion and justice relate to the critical problems facing the contemporary black church?

5. In terms of Christian evangelism, will the faith *have children*?

Issues for Study and Discussion

1. Was it a "dumb or unwise decision" for Sally Harris to get off the search committee? (See Prov 2:1–7)

2. In the Corner Stone Church family, on what biblical basis would you likely ground the authority of spiritual leadership entrusted to a woman called to ministry? (See Prov 9:1–10; Gal. 3:28)

3. In the lived world of experience, what is the most loving thing to do in deciding between a man and woman equally qualified to assume the pastoral office? (See Eph 4:1–15)

4. Why were other members of the search committee, apparently, silent for the most part in the face of controversy? (See Ps 108:1–4; Prov 26:27–28)

5. What is the role of Christian women who virtually fill the pews of local congregations for Sunday morning worship? (See John 3:16; Eph 4:7)

6. Is the power of the pew similar to a "*sleeping giant*"?

7. How can the contemporary church in community overcome the traditional attitude among some people who boasted: "we've always had a male pastor over the flock? (See Acts 10:1–20; Eph. 2:10)

Teaser Test Answer Sheet

Multiple Choice:
True-False:

1. C (Atlanta, Georgia)
1. False
2. D (January 15, 1929)
2. False
3. A (Colgate Rochester Seminary)
3. False
4. B (Tired of the system of segregation)
4. True
5. D (Approximately one year)
5. False
6. B (Rapid Transit System)
6. True
7. B (Ebenezer Baptist Church)
7. False
8. True
9. False
10. True
11. True

Completion:

1. Montgomery, Alabama
   Rosa Parks's refusal to give up her seat to a white man.
   The bus boycott movement.

2. Greensboro, North Carolina
   The beginning of the non-violent "sit-in" protest at Woolworth's by four courageous North Carolina Art College students.

3. Selma, Alabama
   Freedom March from Selma to Montgomery.
   Voting right campaign that gradually ended legal segregation in American public life.

4. Birmingham, Alabama
   The bombing and killing of four little girls in a church.
   Dr. King wrote a letter from the Birmingham jail.

5. Washington, D.C.
   March on Washington.
   Dr. King gave the "*I Have A Dream*" speech.

6. Oslo, Norway
   Dr. King received the Nobel Peace Prize.

7. Memphis, Tennessee
   The garbage strike.
   Dr. King's assassination, April 4, 1968.

Notes

1. Cheryl J. Sanders, ed., *Living The Intersection: Womanism and Afrocentrism in Theology* (Minneapolis: Fortress Press, 1995) 9. Perhaps what is most fascinating about the intellectual development of womanism and Afrocentrism arises from the ways in which it unmasks the biases and limits of Eurocentrism. Hence, the womanist nomenclature provides the African American Christian, in particular, with an alternative worldview. Professor Sanders argues, for instance, that Afrocentric scholarship seeks to do three basic things: (*a*) "celebrate the achievements of African people and culture; (*b*) analyze critically the hegemony of the Eurocentric worldview and ways of knowing that have served the interests of racial oppression, especially as they have skewed the self-understanding of African American educators and leaders; and (*c*) construct an alternative framework for understanding and evaluating human experience," 158.

2. Ibid., 10. It is important to mention that many scholars and black theologians draw striking parallels between Afrocentrism and womanism, since they both emerged as parts of an oppressed people's culture of resistance. They both are designed—pragmatically and intellectually—to correct what the renowned historian Carter G. Woodson called the "mis-education" of African-Americans, given the tragic legacy of centuries of European imperialism and colonialism and the subsequent domination of white over black. Historically, this peculiar reality of European imperialism took its initial economic roots in the establishment of a form of slavery in Jamestown, Virginia, in 1619. So then, the historic struggle of black women *and* men is intrinsic to womanist ethics and ideology. In one sense, "womanist" means black feminist. By unmasking Afrocentric rhetoric, both Rosa Parks and Coretta Scott King are *practical* examples of womanism. Although contemporary scholars such as Jacquelyn Grant, Delores S. Williams, Kelly Brown Douglas, Renita Weems, Katie G. Cannon, Karen Baker-Fletcher—to name only a few—provide the reader with a self-critical theoretical perspective on matters of faith and struggle.

3. David J. Garrow, *Bearing The Cross* (New York: Vintage Books, 1988) 11. The winner of the Pulitzer Prize, this significant volume tells the story of Martin Luther King, Jr., and the Southern Christian Leadership Conference. Provocative as it is complex, Garrow chronicles the valor and courage of women behind the movement—such as Rosa Parks, Coretta Scott King, Mrs. Bertha Butler, Jo Ann Robinson who was President of the Women's Political Council (WPC) of Montgomery, and Claudette Colvin, a 15-year-old high school student who refused a driver's demand to give up her seat so newly boarding whites could sit down. Ironically, this little known incident took place on March 2, 1955 as the vicious hands of white policemen dragged young Colvin from the bus. "Colvin's resistance to the arresting officers," says Garrow, "had resulted in her being charged with assault and battery as well as violating city and state segregation statutes," 15.

4. Ibid., 11.

5. Ibid.

6. Ibid.

7. Ibid.

8. Ibid.

9. Martin Luther King, Jr., *Stride Toward Freedom* (New York: Harper and Row, 1958) 30.

10. Ibid., 28.

11. Ibid., 29.

12. King, 28–37. In the heat of the Montgomery protest movement, we discovered that Dr. King was not only a discerning moral leader and orator, but also a theologian. He utilized the revolutionary story of Mrs. Parks to suggest theologically that "she had been tracked down by the *Zeitgeist*—the spirit of the time," the immutable forces of destiny that neither Rosa Parks nor Coretta Scott King could walk away from. In short, when history speaks, strong women of courage listen.

13. Dr. Benjamin E. Mays, "Commencement Address" (Lane College Graduation Ceremonies, May, 1967: Jackson, Tennessee).

14. Herbert Kohl, *She Would Not Be Moved* (New York: The New Press, 2005) 11. In a very powerful way, Herbert Kohl tells the story of Rosa Parks and the Montgomery Bus Boycott by focusing on its educational possibilities for a whole new generation of children, whose lives have been shaped in the post-Civil Rights era. The book itself is a masterful narrative that has the potential to inspire a generation of young people—both black and white—to embrace the promise of the "American Dream" without losing the integrity of their own ethnic identity. The noted educator and advocate for children, Marian Wright Edelman, wrote the introduction to this book, in which she said the following about Rosa Parks: "I have a special respect for Rosa Parks because I grew up surrounded by women like her in my own hometown of Bennettsville, South Carolina. I was so blessed to grow up in a household with a true partnership between a mother and father . . . Women are quite often the glue that holds together not only our homes, but our congregations, institutions, and communities," (*xv*).

15. E. Hammond Oglesby, *O Lord, Move This Mountain: Racism and Christian Ethics* (St. Louis: Chalice Press, 1998) 79–86. From a religio-ethical perspective in the black church tradition, there is no room for the language of *niggerism*. Metaphorically, I regard it as the "first cousin" to racism in our socio-political system of white domination and control. Unfortunately, given the seduction of modern-day capitalism and greed, many artists of "rap culture" have made "niggerology" or the language of the "bad nigger" their passport to success and fame. Like its first cousin racism, I argue theologically and pragmatically that "niggerism" is dehumanizing and destructive to the moral fabric of the African American community. Like the corrosive evil of sexism, it dehumanizes our women, mothers, daughters, and nieces by reducing them to mere objects of sexual gratification and male dominated power. Theologically discerned, it is important for black folk in America to remember that God did not make us or declare: "*You were born* niggers." Rather the redemptive love of God claims us as God's own children and family. As Holy Scripture affirms: "See how very much our heavenly Father loves us, for he allows us to be called his children, and we really are" (1 John 3:1 NLT)!

16. Douglas Brinkley, *Rosa Parks: A Life* (New York: The Penguin Group, 2000) 11.

17. Ibid., 12.

18. Ibid.

19. Stewart Burns, *To The Mountaintop: Martin Luther King, Jr.'s Sacred Mission to Save America 1955–1968* (New York: Harper Collins Publishers, Inc., 2004) 18.

20. Kevin Chappell, "The Life and Legacy of The Mother of The Civil Rights Movement" (Chicago: Ebony, a Johnson Publication, January, 2006) 130.

21. Chappell, 130.

22. Ibid., 132.

23. Ibid., 127.

24. Kohl, *xiii*.

25. Chappell, 132.

26. Kohl, *xiv*.

27. Chappell, 132.

28. King, 66. Perhaps for both womanist ethics and black theology, the moral insight into King's critical thought arises from his dialectical method of holding in creative tension *particularity*, on the one hand; and the normative element of *universalism*, on the other. By this I mean to suggest that Martin, Coretta, and Rosa Parks held on to "nonviolent resistance"—a philosophy learned from Mahatma Gandhi—as the "technique" of the movement, while the ethic of Christian love stood as the regulating ideal. King reported that in the heat of the initial protest movement, "the phrase most often heard was "Christian love," said King. He further quipped: "It was the sermon on the Mount . . . that initially inspired the Negroes of Montgomery to dignified social action. It was Jesus of Nazareth that stirred the Negroes to protest with the creative weapon of love."

29. Edgar A. Toppin, *A Bibliographical History of Blacks in America Since 1528* (New York: David McKay Company, Inc., 1969) 191.

30. Richard Newman, ed., *African American Quotations* (New York: Checkmark Books, 2000) 92.

31. "Celebrating Her Spirit" (The Commemorative King Family Document, January, 2006) 1.

32. Ibid.

33. Ibid., 1–4.

34. Newman, 390.

35. "Celebrating Her Spirit" (The Commemorative King Family Document, January, 2006), 9.

36. John Lovell, Jr., *Black Song: The Forge and The Flame* (New York: Paragon House Publishers, 1972) 288.

37. Newman, 347.

38. "Celebrating Her Spirit" (The Commemorative King Family Document, January, 2006) 15.

39. Ibid. As a partner in the struggle for justice and peace around the world, Mrs. King devoted her life and moral energy to the full development of the King Center and its noble ideals for all humanity. Atlanta, Georgia is a better place in which to live because of the transforming deeds and womanist spirit of Coretta Scott King. For Coretta, the womanist spirit cannot be limited to the struggles and injustices experienced by black people only. Rather it is a *miraculous spirit* inclusive of, and responsive to, all people who have suffered from the brutality of sexism, racism, and a white male dominated hierarchy in American society. Thus Coretta Scott King knew that a *womanist* is also a *feminist*. For example, the theologian Rosemary Radford Ruether has observed, and I think rightly so, that the term "feminism" is usually understood to mean both a point of view and a social movement that stresses the equality of women. "Feminism affirms the equivalent human personhood of women," says Ruether, "and seeks to overcome the disabilities of women in culture . . . that have been shaped by male domination." (Source – Unpublished paper: "Feminism as a New World View," Northwestern University). In short, it is my strong conviction that Coretta

Scott King, Rosa Parks, and Mary McLeod Bethune reflected feminism in a new key. If not, why not? If not their legacy, whose legacy? Pressing toward the mark means—in one sense—seeing ourselves as "fresh fruits" of their legacy.

40. Ibid. It is an amazingly beautiful thing that Bernice A. King, a minister of the gospel of Jesus Christ, followed in the footsteps of her famous father. She is a seminary graduate of Candler School of Theology, Emory University, Atlanta, Georgia. In terms of intellectual productivity, Rev. Bernice A. King wrote the forward to Noel Leo Erskine's book, *King Among the Theologians* (Cleveland: The Pilgrim Press, 1994). Bernice is keenly aware that womanist ethics and theology provide a constructive critique of black church life and its largely male dominated leadership. To be sure, her own mother—Coretta Scott King—represents an important bridge of strength, mutuality, equality, intelligence, and courage between black women and black men in society today. At the celebrative memorial, Rev. Bernice King said this about her mother: "I learned from the last three months of my mother's life the value of moments."

41. Ibid., 15–16cf.

42. Cited in William R. Miller, *Martin Luther King, Jr.: His Life, Martyrdom and Meaning For the World* (New York: Avon Books, 1968) 66. While the principle of love may require greater theoretical and ethical clarity for the oppressed, King used it as an instrument in search of authentic freedom, justice, and reconciliation in a conflicted world of bigotry and violence. In the heart of his social ethic—with a *womanist* inclination—I think that Martin and Coretta fought hard against the tragic evils of racism, war, and poverty. These were core moral themes in the public life of both individuals as icons in the African American Christian community.

43. E. Hammond Oglesby, *Ethics and Theology From the Other Side: Sounds of Moral Struggle* (Washington, D.C.: University Press of America, Inc., 1979) 121cf.

44. Ibid., 121.

45. Coretta Scott King, *My Life With Martin Luther King, Jr.* (New York: Avon Books, 1969) 135.

46. Ibid.

47. Ibid. I strongly believe that Christian ethics for the black church today must be the sort of *ethic* that celebrates the rich legacy of Coretta Scott, Rosa Parks, and Martin Luther King, Jr. Indeed, while there were many other nameless warriors of "justice and peace" during the Civil Rights era, these icons symbolize the best in the value system of the American Democratic Republic. They wanted us to "stand up for righteousness." As a social ethicist, it is a peculiar irony to note that it was a Republican president in the White House, Ronald Reagan, who signed the document in 1986 declaring the birthday of Martin Luther King, Jr. a national holiday. "What is the meaning of this symbolic political act for African American voters?" The discerning and morally sensitive Christian is prone to wonder. To be sure, throughout this chapter I have argued that Coretta and Martin worked in *partnership* in the struggle for freedom, justice, and racial equality. Given the diverse political narratives that floated around the memorial celebration of Coretta Scott King, it is interesting to note that President Bush gave this appropriate tribute:

Our Nation is deeply saddened by the death of Coretta Scott King. Mrs. King was a beloved, graceful, and courageous woman who called America to its founding ideals and carried on a noble dream. She was a great Civil Rights leader, and her contributions to freedom and equality made America a better and more compassionate nation. The United States of America is grateful for the good life of Coretta Scott King.

Laura and I were honored to have known Mrs. King, and we will always treasure the time we spent with her. On behalf of all Americans, we send our prayers and heartfelt sympathy to the family and friends of Coretta Scott King.

48. Andrew Young, "The Untold Story of Martin Luther King, Jr. and Coretta Scott King" (Ebony, a Johnson publication, April, 2006) 184 cf.

49. "Celebrating Her Spirit" (The Commemorative King Family Document, January, 2006) 26cf.

Chapter Four

Pressing Toward the Mark
What's in Your Bucket?

Liberation means you don't have to be silenced.
— Toni Morrison, 1931
Novelist and Nobel Laureate

I press on toward the goal for the prize
of the heavenly call of God in Christ Jesus . . .
Only let us hold fast to what we have attained.
—Philippians 3:14–16

T HE DEEP stories of the Bible know nothing of solitary saints or spiritual hermits isolated from the toils and trials, and the hopes and dreams of the community. *Pressing toward the mark* requires not a solitary act of bravery, but a communal act of faith. *Pressing toward the mark* is a figure of ethical speech that rejects the "lone ranger" image of rugged individualism or pulpit-egoism that dominate some of our churches in the black community today. *Pressing toward the mark* requires compassion over competition in the body politic of the black religious community. Indeed, the ethical speech of pressing toward the mark as Christian believers means that we come together as God's family to build bridges rather than walls; to build together bridges of understanding and possibility, which can set us free from those things that so easily enslave us in our culture. *Pressing toward the mark*, therefore, as members of God's own family, puts the ethic of we-consciousness back into what it means to be *Christian* in the first place. Existentially, I think that part of the reality implicit in we-consciousness is the paradox of *bearing one another's burdens* yet, every child of God is responsible for bearing his or her own burdens (Gal 6:5). For Christians, the burden of the word of the Lord is ever upon our lips, especially in the search for the common good. Central to the theme of pressing toward the mark,

Matthew 11:29–30 depict a compassionate Jesus giving us all a simple invitation:

> Take my yoke upon you, and learn from me; for I am gentle and humble in heart, and you will find rest for your souls. For my yoke is easy, and my burden is light.

In the context of the Christian moral life, God—as disclosed in the personality of Jesus—loves to use ordinary people, warts and all, to do extraordinary things. Remember the principle advocated by elders in the black religious community, that ordinary ability among humans becomes extraordinary under the protective wings of God. Once we surrender to God's will as Christian believers and moral agents of the way, we allow God to use us according to God's will for our lives. In a word, we learn to be happy with the "yoke" of Christian discipleship. There is no profound mystery in regard to the moral imperative to follow Jesus: "take my yoke upon you and learn from me . . . for my yoke is easy, and my burden is light" (Matt 11:29). It is interesting to note that *Webster's New World Dictionary* defines the term "yoke" as "a wooden frame for harnessing together a pair of oxen." For Christian ethics in black church life, the notion of a "yoke" implies that the faithful believer is drawn to that which *binds* and *unites* people in the common struggle for liberation and empowerment. To be "yoked" means to be fitted for the journey by putting on the proper garment. Ethically, the act of "yoking" is an invitation on the part of the believer to "join together" for a greater good. Therefore, it is my fundamental moral conviction that *pressing toward the mark* is a pastoral and prophetic act of "yoking."

Given the particularity of this chapter, the notion of *pressing toward the mark* has grown out of the interaction of two convictions. The first is the deep conviction that faithfulness to one another—in the complex web of human relationships—is critical to an Afrocentric Christian outlook on the moral life and the black religious experience in America. For my own conceptual framework, I propose the use of a *covenant-harambee* model of ethical discourse. I will say more about that later in this chapter. The second conviction is that the contemporary black church has an inescapable obligation to speak to critical life and death issues confronting our children, adolescents, young adults, and other people of color in society—especially where sexism, racism, and classism still afflict us all.

In this last chapter therefore, we shall briefly focus some attention upon the following concerns: the search for a viable method of moral discourse, a careful look at three nagging social problems that require moral agency on the part of the contemporary black church today, and the uses of the Bible in black church life. We shall also invite the reader to engage in a process of critical discussion and self-reflection on twelve "moral laws" that may impact our social behavior in pressing toward the mark—especially in terms of their potential application to case studies we have included. As Christian believers, let us now go to what I regard as a reasonable method of moral discourse.

Method of Moral Discourse

In the context of the black church tradition, it is my conviction that those who do Christian ethics in our society today must explore an alternative approach to the moral life. As Christian believers, this approach must be, necessarily, different from previous patterns of ethical reasoning such as utilitarianism, relativism, hedonism, or rugged individualism—many of which are so common in our secular culture. The selection of a model in ethical discourse is therefore, a *defining moment* in the life of persons shaped by values and beliefs inherent in the black church tradition.

For example, the authors Tom Rath and Donald O. Clifton, in their national bestseller *How Full is Your Bucket?* raised with the ethically sensitive reader, some of the important issues in regard to positive strategies toward life, work, and faith.[1] An Afrocentric Christian outlook strongly affirms that we become ethical not by *chance*, but by *choice*—in one's struggle to press toward the mark. Since ethics, logically, can be defined as a process of self-critical reflection about the *choices* we make, and how they impact our values and faith journey, we as moral agents not only struggle with the question, What will God have me to do and be? but also the metaphorical question, What's in your bucket as a follower of Christ? Ethically, the question raised here is also deeply personal and pragmatic, namely: *What's in my bucket?* In their analysis, Rath and Clifton argued that the concept of the bucket could be understood in the following manner:

> Each of us has an invisible bucket. It is constantly emptied or filled, depending on what others say or do to us. When our bucket is full, we feel great. When it's empty, we feel awful.

> Each of us also has an invisible dipper. When we use that dipper to fill other people's buckets — by saying or doing things to increase their positive emotions — we also fill our own bucket. But when we use that dipper to dip from others' buckets — by saying or doing thing that decrease their positive emotions — we diminish ourselves.[2]

For Christians, the image of an "invisible bucket" is reflective of the empowering grace of God in, and over, our lives, which gives us strength for today and hope for tomorrow. For many decades, the black church tradition has taught us that each human being is a person of worth, a child of God possessing certain strengths, virtues, and abilities to fill our "buckets" with positive spiritual gifts (1 Cor 14:1), in order that we may be zealous in following the Christian moral life (Eph 4:8). When our bucket is full, we feel great. When it's empty, we feel awful. Accordingly the critical ethical question tugging at our conscience is simply this: What should I, as a believer in Jesus Christ and member of his church, have in my bucket? It seems to me that a lot could be riding on how the contemporary black church in society responds to this probing ethical question. As a community of the Spirit, one's "invisible dipper" and bucket must come together for the common good in our world. While our choices are often murky and morally ambiguous in life, Rath and Clifton further proclaimed:

> Like the cup that runneth over, a full bucket gives us a positive outlook and renewed energy. Every drop in that bucket makes us stronger and more optimistic.

> But an empty bucket poisons our outlook, saps our energy, and undermines our will. That's why, every time someone dips from our bucket, it hurts us.

> So we face a choice every moment of every day: We can fill one another's buckets, or we can dip from them. It's an important choice—one that profoundly influences our relationships, productivity, health, and happiness.[3]

Ethically discerned, the bottom line, for both Tom Rath and Donald O. Clifton, is the self-awareness that we are at our best when our buckets are overflowing with good things—and at our worst when they are empty. For the Christian, everyone has an "invisible dipper," which I recognize as the revolutionary power of the Spirit, ever present in the throes and struggles of African Americans and other people of color throughout the history of our nation. The black church tradition affirms that the Holy Spirit teaches us. The Holy Spirit leads us. The Holy Spirit liberates and heals the deep wounds we suffer in life—as a covenant people possessing a variety of gifts. As Holy Scripture affirms: "Now there are varieties of gifts, but the same Spirit; and there are varieties of services, but the same Lord; and there are varieties of activities, but it is the same God who activates all of them in everyone" (1 Cor 12:4–6).

In terms of a viable method of moral discourse, I am proposing what I call a *covenant-harambee* approach as an outgrowth of the bucket imagery. For example, in the context of the Christian moral life in the black church, do we take time out to explore meaningful bucket filling within ourselves, or others? What we recognize in ourselves, or others, is the need for spiritual and moral guidance—if we are to press toward the mark and lay hold on future accomplishments. In the context of covenant relationships therefore, "bucket filling" must be specific to the cultural identity and values of the individual.

For this reason but not this reason only, the ancient Socratic principle, "the unexamined life is not worth living," is important for every African American Christian to remember. Not sure where to go from here? Just ask yourself some questions. What's in my own bucket as a Christian or follower of Christ? Is jealousy or envy of others in my bucket? Is low self-esteem in my bucket? Is fear or misplaced anxiety in my bucket? Is the philosophy of "keeping-up-with-the-Joneses" in my bucket? Could it be possible that the negative attitude of *poor little me* has slipped into my bucket? What about the sins of omission and commission lodged in my bucket? What positive emotion or energy fills your bucket the most? What biblical stories or words from the gospel tradition seem to fill your bucket and bring hope? How can God's justice and peace fit into our buckets as we press toward the mark? Given the gravity of these questions, one of the deep moral lessons to be learned here on the part of the Christian believer arises from the fact that whenever we choose to fill others' buckets, we in turn fill our own. Hence, the rag-tag ethic of "bucket-filling" is a game of hospitality and mutuality. Put another way, when we lose ourselves in service to God and others, we also find our true purpose and ourselves.

Indeed, this is the profound irony and beauty implicit in the stories of Rosa Parks, Coretta Scott King, and Mary McLeod Bethune, to name only a few. In retrospect, they all had something *special* in their buckets as a means of coping with the trials and tribulations of life. Now in terms of moral discourse in particular, I am suggesting the covenant-harambee model as something worth having in one's bucket, with respect to the critical issues facing the contemporary black church in America. Accordingly, let us take a closer look at the covenant-harambee model.

For example, Joseph L. Allen, in his book *Love and Conflict: A Covenantal Model of Christian Ethics*, rightly observes that "sometimes ethicists adopt a model without announcing to their readers (or even to themselves) that they have done so, but the model's influence over their theory is no less pervasive.[4] As a Christian ethicist, I do not wish to be found guilty of the sin of omission in this regard. Therefore, I declare a sort of an inherent positive bias toward "covenant," in one's attempt to press toward the mark in the moral life of the black church tradition. The Hebrew word for covenant, *berit*, denotes an "obligation" or "binding claim" upon the believer or moral agent in the life and faith of the church. From an Afrocentric perspective, a pivotal passage that illustrates this point is Micah 6:8: "And what does the Lord require of you but to do justice, and to love kindness, and to walk humbly with your God?" The relationship of covenant and "divine commands" is illustrated over and over again in the prophetic tradition of the Bible, especially the prophet Amos, who was a normative icon for the work and ministry of Martin Luther King, Jr. But the morally sensitive person must, necessarily, ask: What is the nature of a covenant relationship? Here Professor Joseph L. Allen further asserts:

> A covenant relationship comes about through interactions of entrusting and accepting entrustment. A covenant is not simply a biological relationship, like that of brother and sister, though a biological relationship may for other reasons also be covenantal. Nor is it merely happenstance, as geographical proximity may be. Rather a covenant comes into being as people, whether they are closely related biologically or geographically or not, entrust themselves to one another and correspondingly accept one another's entrustment.[5]

The very nature of a covenant relationship involves *entrustment*, faith, and the love of justice on the part of the Christian believer in the black church tradition. Specifically, Allen uses the concept of *entrustment* to suggest that a genuine covenant relationship "comes about through interactions of entrusting and accepting entrustment among willing, personal beings . . . as a result, the parties belong to the same moral community and have responsibility to and for one another as beings who matter . . . ."[6] Comparatively a parallel concept in the black religious tradition is the notion *leaning on Jesus*. For a people with a deep history of pain and oppression in America, the idea of a life without Jesus is like a day without sunshine for African American Christians in the black church.

The sheer activity of *leaning on Jesus* reflects two elementary virtues on the part of the believer: (*a*) Jesus as a moral source of strength who liberates and reconciles; and (*b*) Jesus as a spiritual source of strength who heals and snatches our lives from the edge of the "pit"—in order that we may press toward the mark. In the light of these virtues, the functions of Jesus, in a covenant-harambee model, are far-reaching in the black church tradition. For example, the relational concepts of entrustment and *leaning on Jesus* can be further illustrated in the Afro-American Spiritual, "*Ride on King Jesus!*"

Many black people in contemporary society today will tell you that the ultimate and final source of their power is Jesus. "In the morning, noon, or night . . . I go to Jesus, He makes everything alright," shouted one elderly mother of the black church. Hence the notion of "King Jesus" is one who performs all manner of good things under difficult circumstances. A few verses from the song, "*Ride on King Jesus*," reflects this miraculous and creative power:

> When I was blind and could not see,
> King Jesus brought that light to me.
> When every star refuses to shine, . . .
> I know King Jesus will be mine.
>
> He is King of Kings, He is Lord of Lords,
> Jesus Christ the first and last,
> No man works like him.
> He pitched his tents on Canaan's ground,
> And broke the Roman Kingdom down.[7]

As a people of faith, Christian ethics in the black church tradition affirms "King Jesus"—arising from a covenant-harambee model—who not only saves us, but brings light from darkness: that is to say, "when every star refuses to shine . . . I know King Jesus will be mine."

In the volume *O Lord, Move This Mountain*, I have agonized over an alternative ethical model that I have described as the covenant-harambee approach. Such an African concept of harambee bears affinity to the Hebraic-Christian notion of covenant. Comparatively, the two conceptual elements, harambee and covenant, seem to form a viable perspective for understanding and exploring the spiritual sources of Christian ethics—especially in a world where the deep moral issues of faith and culture, identity and freedom, pastoral authority and self-integrity cry out for dialogue and response in black church life. Now as a method of ethical discourse I wish to develop further, theoretically, a covenant-harambee approach in addressing critical issues of human society.[8]

Concretely, the basic idea of *harambee* in the ethics and religion of traditional African society has come to mean "pulling together," "hanging together," and "solidarity" in the struggle for the common good. For a multi-cultural and religiously diverse people, harambee has come to mean a "walking together" upon this earth in the spirit of God's love and righteousness.[9] The idea of harambee for women and men of faith is all about how we can act in social solidarity to see the church as one body—bearing prophetic witness in our time. For example, the notion of harambee was first used in the rituals and ceremonies of East African culture as a symbolic call to unity and collective struggle among suffering and oppressed people, and later it was adopted in the mid-1960s as a symbol of moral empowerment. Historically speaking, Maulana Karenga, in his book *Kwanzaa: A Celebration of Family and Community and Culture*, describes the manner in which the concept of harambee evolved ethically and culturally in the black community of America. Here he empathically proclaims harambee as a dynamic religio-cultural activity of the head and heart:

Another activity and reinforcing gesture is the Harambee, which is a call to unity and collective work and struggle. We of the Organization Us took the call itself from a practice in East Africa in 1965 and added to the verbal call the raising of the right arm with open hand and pulling down and closing our hand into a fist at the same time. This was done for two reasons. First, it was to simulate the raised power fist, which was at the time a basic Black Power symbol. Secondly, it was done because the work "Harambee" was a chant continent Africans used when pulling and thus, its general meaning is "let's all pull together." Also, Harambee are usually done in sets of seven in honor and reinforcement of the Nguzo Saba, and may be done at anytime to urge unity and collective work and struggle.[10]

In the broader moral context of the black church tradition, the notion of harambee is an engaging paradigm that provides the most authoritative source for understanding the values, beliefs, mores, and spiritual practices of African people around the world. Reaffirming the integrity, beauty, and dynamism of human life, the notion of harambee fosters a unitive thread of religion and ethics, on the one hand; and it engenders a balanced combination of liturgy and social protest on the other.[11]

For example, the Afrocentric notion of harambee challenges us all in the contemporary black church to press toward the mark. Theologically, it is impossible to discuss a covenant-harambee model of moral discourse apart from faith in God and the love of justice. For example, in the biblical narrative, God's liberating grace initiates, sustains, and continually renews the covenant relationship. Though brokenness, suffering, and pain seem to easily characterize our contemporary world, God steadfastly yearns that we embrace the full fellowship in the covenant community.

Therefore, the covenant-harambee model sets forth a basic standard of "we-consciousness" and obedience to God's command, in terms of our behavior one to another (Deut 6:5; Amos 5:7; Luke 19:5). For Christian ethics in the black church tradition, "we-consciousness" is a way of saying that individual identity is socially connected with others in human community. To be sure, there is an African proverb that expresses this relationship nicely. It reads: "I am because we are, and since we are, therefore, I am." We shall now look at the "cry for justice" as a one of the ingredients in one's bucket, in the attempt to better understand critical or nagging issues today.

The Cry for Justice: Three Nagging Issues

Of all the biblical and theological themes that we have unpacked so far in our discussion on the black moral tradition, there is none more relevant than the theme of God's justice. Thus, we must seek to discern what kind of justice that God demands that we have. The biblical word is that God's justice is inseparable from God's love and compassion, that God's justice is a liberating and saving justice, that God's justice lifts up the fallen, cares for the helpless, empowers the powerless, and restores human community.

Drawing on the biblical witness to God's justice and other theological convictions about God, our neighbors, and ourselves we may postulate six guidelines for moral action. Faithfulness to the God of justice, we know, requires us to: (*a*) show equal respect and concern for all; (*b*) demonstrate special concern for the poor and oppressed; (*c*) respond to human needs; (*d*) respect human freedom; (*e*) contribute to the well-being of the community; and (*f*) press toward the mark implied in the concept of the "beloved community," as expressive of the ethical vision of Martin Luther King, Jr. for the future of the church.

How do we respond to the call of God to serve the cause of justice in our particular churches and communities? What things must be in our buckets for Jesus? In the first place, *we need to learn as much as we can about what is going on in the world.* In the contemporary black church today, I believe that an uncritical faith is no substitute for facts. Theology is no substitute for social analysis. Good intentions are of little value if we don't know what in the world is going on. If we are to serve God in our particular historical context, our time and place in history, we need to understand our context. This doesn't mean—thank God—that we have all got to become economists or political scientists! But it does mean that we have all got to do some homework. Avoidable ignorance is no excuse. Selective amnesia is not allowed.

How, then, can we make sense out of three of the most agonizing issues confronting the black church community today, namely: (*a*) the growing AIDS epidemic in the black community; (*b*) the absence of a robust youth involvement, male and female, in the total life of the contemporary church; and (*c*) the perennial and nagging problem of racism in our society? As we continue to ponder the wider pragmatic question of this chapter, "*What's in your bucket?*" the cry for justice demands that pastors, Christian educators, parents, and community leaders respond to these critical issues. To engage in ethics in a Christian context means that the community must respond to human needs. The gospel tradition: for instance, reminds us all of the imperative: that "when I was hungry, you gave me food; thirsty, you gave me water; naked, you gave me clothing" (Matt 25:35). The moral agent affirms 1 Timothy 6:8: "having food and raiment let us be content." Therefore, to be ethical means to respond to human need and the cry for justice in our society today.

In the second place, *we need to become more sensitive to the immediate need of persons around us and to engage in ministries of compassion.* In the black church tradition, a ministry of compassion is oriented around God's justice and mercy. What, then, is God's justice in relation to the AIDS epidemic, our youth, and racism in modern society today? Ethically discerned, the idea of justice means giving to each his or her due. For example, in our competitive economy in America, a theology of economic justice means "fair wages" for a fair day's work, regardless of race, class, color, gender, or sexual orientation. Here a theology of economic justice means that each human being must have what it takes to sustain life, at a human level—one that reflects freedom and dignity in community. I suspect that Christian ethics in the black church tradition was, inevitably, about *survival* and faith in a God who is just. In a broader sense, this means that churches in local black communities must engage in conversation, in terms of sustaining life at a more human level, regarding: (*a*) the dilemmas of the job market and economic empowerment; indeed, the case study in this chapter highlights these concerns for the ethically sensitive person; (*b*) sustaining life at a more human level involves the church as a family support system; (*c*) the power to see the church as a community of moral discourse and action; and the reality of sustaining life at a more human level involves pressing toward the mark of God's justice for the hurting ones and marginalized in our world today.

God's justice therefore, is the power of God's love to show compassion toward the broken and alienated ones in our community. God's justice is a staff of mercy that goes the *second mile* for the hurting ones in our midst. To love God means to do *justice*, I think, in relationship to the AIDS epidemic in black community. There is no *nagging* issue more critical on the contemporary American scene—impacting the lives of mothers, babies, fathers, sons, daughters, and teenage friends—of which the leadership in the black church must respond than the issue of AIDS. For example, the World Health Organization reports that since the first cases of acquired immunodeficiency syndrome (AIDS) were reported in 1981, human immunodeficiency virus (HIV) has grown to pandemic proportions, resulting in an estimated 65 million infections and 25 million deaths.

According to the Centers for Disease Control and Prevention, there are an estimated 1.039 million to 1.185 million HIV-positive individuals living in the United States—the largest number ever. Of these, between 252,000 and 315,000 people do not know they are infected, and thus are suffering from a lack of treatment. Later, many individuals who become aware suffer from fear, silence, shame, and often rejection by both family and community. In terms of ethnic variables, nearly one half of new cases reported each year in the U.S. are African American. According to Shelly A. Schneider, a noted journalist, Americans should be reminded that HIV/AIDS does not discriminate. With an estimated 1,039,000 to 1,185,000 HIV-positive individuals living in the U.S. and 35,000 to 40,000 new infections occurring every year, the U.S., like other nations around the world, is deeply affected by HIV/AIDS.

In a multicultural and multiracial society where the whisper of the word "AIDS" usually sends chills up the spine of ordinary people, the real ethical question confronting the Christian community is simple as it is awesome: *Can the Church find her voice?* For many people in our time, the AIDS epidemic is like a powerful demonic tidal wave crashing the shores of cities, poverty stricken villages, and nations. In its wake it leaves behind a misty cloud of death, destruction, social abandonment and fear—as morally reasonable persons scramble to respond to this critical dilemma.[12] In some quarters of what Robert McAfee Brown calls the "global village," the AIDS epidemic is, metaphorically considered, sort of like one's attempt to climb a treacherous mountain in the dead of winter without being adequately equipped with proper clothing and technical gear. Whatever metaphor or illustration one might use in modern society, AIDS challenges the church universal to find her voice and to respond to complex ethical, religious, and cultural issues in the light of one's personal needs.[13] For morally reasonable persons, it is a profound understanding to suggest that the church has experienced incredible difficulty in finding her own voice or her peculiar spiritual rhythm in response to the problem of AIDS. Viewed accordingly, Kenneth R. Overberg, in his book *AIDS,*

Ethics and Religion, has carefully nuanced the worsening crisis of AIDS and the church's mixed response to it. He puts the matter this way:

> AIDS . . . challenges religion to respond to complex ethical and societal issues and to profound, personal needs. The response has been mixed. Representatives of some religions have described AIDS as God's punishment for sexual sin. Some people have attempted to nuance their reactions, judging some actions as evil but also helping people in need. Still others have stressed the need to commit people and resources to compassionate care for all people with AIDS.[14]

As an ethical theologian, Overberg is quick to point out that the tragic reality of AIDS is that it touches all dimensions of life and thereby challenges us to remember that AIDS is *our* disease, a painful and alienation-oriented disease of the human family. Yet within the Christian community the forces of faith and conscience call us to clarify the hard questions and moral dilemmas.

For some African American Christians, one of the moral dilemmas—besides shame—is the reality of not facing the hard facts about the AIDS epidemic in America. Here it is my conviction that black churches today need to share with its members the difficult and hard data about AIDS itself. For example, the most recent data available on racial/ethnic distribution of female adolescent AIDS cases are from 1998. These data reveal that most female adolescent cases occurred among racial/ethnic minorities. In 1998, 447/688 (65%) female AIDS cases among 13–24 year olds were black, not Hispanic, 110/688 (16%) were Hispanic, and 123/688 (18%) were white, not Hispanic.[15] William J. Cromie, in a recent article entitled, "*AIDS Epidemic Called Crisis Among Blacks*," has pointed out to the whole community that from 1985 until 1996, whites accounted for the highest percentage of AIDS infections, but the line was crossed in 1996. Cases among whites dropped from 60 percent of the total in 1985 to about 35 percent in 1997. Among blacks, cases have almost doubled, from about 25 percent to 45 percent, in the same period.[16]

> During 1996 and the first half of 1997, the incidence of AIDS fell for the first time in this country. But it didn't fall equally. In 1996–1997 AIDS among whites dropped 23 percent, but among blacks it decreased only 5.6 percent. These statistics were brought out during a two-day meeting at Harvard one week called "The Untold Story: AIDS and Black Americans." It was co-sponsored by the Harvard AIDS institute, the Kaiser Family Foundation, and Leading for Life, a black activist organization.[17]

At a press conference in conjunction with the meeting, Henry Louis Gates, Jr., director of the W.E.B. DuBois Institute for Afro-American Research, summed up the situation this way: "While blacks make up only 12 percent of the U.S. population they account for almost half of the cases of AIDS."[18]

Ethically considered, the hard data also reveals that "dirty" needles play a critical role in contracting AIDS.

One in every two blacks has been tested for infection with HIV—the AIDS virus—compared with 38 percent of all Americans. Among blacks younger than 30 years the testing rate is 65 percent.

Most women, black and white, have contracted AIDS either through illegal drug use (about 45 percent) or heterosexual contact (about 38 percent). Many of the latter cases are due to having sex with men who have gotten the disease from contaminated needles.[19]

The bottom line, I think, revolves around the challenge on the part of black churches in the community to develop spiritual resources and strategies of preventive education with respect to the AIDS epidemic. For example, in mid-1980s, the spiritual resources of the church was powerfully illustrated on the question of AIDS by the Catholic bishops of the United States in two major statements: "*The Many Faces of AIDS: A Gospel Response*," and "*Called to Compassion and Responsibility: A Response to the HIV/AIDS Crisis*" (1989). Now as a result of intense theological debate and ethical discussion about the AIDS crisis, the bishops themselves found moral common ground as they drew the following six major conclusions:

1. AIDS is a human illness, not restricted to one group or social class. AIDS is an ominous presence, calling for the best possible response from the medical and scientific communities.

2. Members of the church have the responsibility to reach out with compassion and understanding to those suffering from AIDS.

3. The crisis demands of the church a clear presentation of its moral teaching concerning human sexuality. Throughout the document, the bishops stress that the only true response to the crisis includes behavior rooted in the fully integrated understanding of human sexuality that grounds the church's teaching.

4. Discrimination against persons with AIDS is unjust and immoral.

5. Society needs to develop appropriate programs, especially educational ones, to prevent the spread of AIDS. A long appendix to the document gives many specific suggestions concerning these programs.

6. Those who are HIV positive ought to live in a way that does not expose others to the disease.[20]

In the third place, Christian ethics for the contemporary black church must attempt to provide greater understanding in regard to a growing absence of youth involvement, male and female, in the total life of the faith community. At times, it seems that a "hip-hop" model among our youth has more appeal than a "discipleship model" as advocated by the gospel of Jesus Christ. Here we must ask, What is a discipleship model? Jesus simply admonished his disciples—by the force of his own personality—"Follow Me" (Matt 4:19), and I will make you "fishers" of men (and women and boys and girls) whose eyes are fixed to the prize of freedom, justice, and equality, without which there can be no true effort to press toward the mark.

> . . . the call to "discipleship"—as compelling image for youth ministry—is the impulse to create meaning for ourselves and others in a world fragmented by a sense of meaninglessness and alienation. The call to Christian discipleship in our culture of consumption and greed goes against the grain of secular humanism and relativism, where there are, apparently, no immediate spiritual and moral boundaries to guide our young people. The call to "discipleship" on the part of youth and adult Christians is an invitation to affirm moral boundaries—often in the absence of useful boundaries in the home, the church, and the wider community. The call to "discipleship" is the impulse to follow Jesus of Nazareth, who reminded his contemporaries: "I am the way, and the truth, and the life. No one comes to the Father except through me" (John 14:6 NRSV). For youth and adults alike, the call to discipleship is an existential one. That is to say that the condition sine quo non of discipleship is the impulse to follow as individuals the lead of the Holy Spirit as revealed in the human community, and through the proclamation of the gospel of Jesus Christ.[21]

By contrast, it is important to note that some religious leaders in the black community are suspicious of the "hip-hop" model, because of its tendency toward negativity in certain aspects of the music industry. To put the matter bluntly: "rap culture" in urban America impacts the rhythmic flux of "church culture" in the religious world—either positively or negatively. Like sexism in our society, negative lyrics emanating from the cultural fabric of the black community dehumanizes our women, mothers, and daughters by reducing them to mere objects of sexual gratification and black male fantasy.

It seems to me that vile, loathsome, and vulgar lyrics offend the moral sensibility of decent human beings anywhere, whether they are black or white, old or young, churched or unchurched. In the stern words of Jesse Jackson, a Christian humanist and noted civil rights advocate: "Black people in general . . . and our youth in particular, have turned on each other rather than to each other in love and respect." For this reason, I think, but not this reason only we have an *absence* of sustained youth involvement in the total life of the contemporary black church in America.

For example, the most mind boggling issue to challenge traditional patterns of leadership in the African American religious community is the conspicuous absence of the black male in the pew. Accordingly, a little voice whispers inside of me: Where are the black males in relation to the mission of the black church? What can hold back the tide of the African American male ecclesial exodus? What is the role of the contemporary black church, in light of the incredible legacies of Mary McLeod Bethune, Rosa Parks, Coretta Scott King, and Martin Luther King, Jr.? As followers of Christ, what do we, in our time, bear witness to? What sources of biblical authority can assist us in pressing toward the mark? For pastors and lay leaders of the church, these questions are important for us to ponder and discuss with family, friends, and members of the household of faith.

A recent study was done that examined the complexity of Christian ethics and black church life, in terms of the absence of the black male in the pew. For example, Calvin Thomas III has written a critical essay entitled, "An Ecclesial Response: The Young African American Male Exodus." Here Thomas documents some of the trends in society that impact the exodus of black males from the church. Sociologically, these trends are inclusive of the fact that African Americans are roughly 12% of the U. S. population, but African American males are 46.5% of the state prison population and 37.8% of the federal prison; and this trend is on the rise. Thomas further points out that, "African American males are arrested at a rate of 28.6% which is twice the African American population."[22] Moreover, the author of this study uncovered the riveting fact that the "African American population has a poverty rate of 23.6% which is greater than twice that of whites, which is 9.8%. The poverty rate for African American children is 39%, which is greater than twice of whites of 15.5%. African American males are being born into households headed by their mothers at a rate of 69.8%. Even more starling, is the rate of African American females going to college with a 3 to 1 ratio to African American males. At some schools, African American females are receiving 65% of bachelor degrees.[23] It seems to me, ethically speaking, that the upshot of these concerns is the challenge that lies ahead for the contemporary black church.

In the fourth place, the cry for justice in the marketplace of our common life is the lamenting cry against the scandal of racism in our society. For many religious leaders, theologians, community activists, and ordinary people of goodwill—this is not a *new lament*, but an old "lamenting cry"—going back to the days when the first African slave was brutally snatched from the familiar places, smells, sights, and sounds of Mother Africa. A "crying lament" in the black church tradition involved a ritual of faith that boldly proclaimed amid the throes of suffering and oppression in America: *"I don't know what the future holds, but I know who holds the future!"*

A crying lament against racism challenges the members of the contemporary black church today not to ever forget our forebears who were once slaves; who endured the trauma of the "Middle Passage;" who landed in Jamestown, Virginia in 1619; and who gallantly fought—by God's grace—to win the prize of freedom from their white oppressors. I strongly believe that it is in the mystery and power of God's grace that people of African descent largely survived the brutality of slavery and the scandal of white racism in American society. Yet racism is a peculiar and continuing reality in our social structure today. White racism is what Derrick Bell, in his national bestseller *Faces at the Bottom of the Well*, called a "permanent reality" in the American socio-cultural system. Those who embrace ethics in the black church tradition must ask the nagging question on the hearts of many folks today, namely: *What is the real difference between prejudice and racism?* Accordingly, I strongly believe that Joseph Barndt's volume, *Dismantling Racism: The Challenge to White America*, goes a long way in helping us to answer this menacing question. He argues for the distinction in this manner:

> Everyone is prejudiced, but not everyone is racist. To be prejudiced means to have opinions without knowing the facts . . . to be racially prejudiced means to have distorted opinions about people of other races. Racism goes beyond prejudice. It is backed up by power. Racism is the power to enforce one's prejudices . . . [24]

Pastors and lay leaders of the church are challenged to remember that—without rethinking the "power equation" in black-white relations—the Christian message of love, justice, and reconciliation loses its vitality. And, therefore, the seriousness of racism as a nagging issue in our society cannot be adequately addressed outside of the question: Who or what holds the power? Ethically considered, power is the capacity to achieve purpose. Power can be good or bad, depending on how it is morally used. Be that as it may, African American Christians and other people of good-will must participate equally in a greater sharing of *power* in all the political, social, and economic institutions of American life. In a negative scenario, Joseph Barndt defines racism as prejudice plus power. Any member of a given ethnic group can, in fact, be prejudiced. "Prejudice" means pre-judgment which leads to mis-judgment, whether that person be Euro-American, Asian, Latino, Native American, or African American. Among the painful results of racism in our society today stems from the fact that it gives rise to *unearned white privilege.*

For example, when I served on the faculty of the Interdenominational Theological Center, in Atlanta, Georgia, as Professor of Christian Ethics, there was an incident that happened to me—which illustrates the residual problem of racism. The gravity of the story involved me receiving a special invitation to join a selected group of people to participate in a new time-share program, located in an incredible resort area approximately 50 miles south of Atlanta. Naturally, I was excited about this new venture or opportunity. I immediately decided to go. To my surprise, I was the only African American in a group of about 20 Euro-Americans—as we sat around a large conference room table to engage in conversation. Suddenly, a slim tall white man, who looked to be in his mid-thirties, stood up in the room and shouted: "I didn't come all the way up here—from Macon, Georgia— to listen to you folks . . . talk about some new timeshare program in a room with a nigger!" These words that fell from this stranger's lips first angered me; then, they hurt me. Racism is pain. Racism is anguish of the human spirit. The sin of racism is grounded in man's basic insecurity. With this incident and countless others suffered by people of color in America, it is the power of white privilege and its legitimating norms, which allowed this white person to stand up in a company of strangers and make such a vile and vulgar declaration.

I suspect for this particular racist, it did not matter that I had achieved the rank of a seminary professor; that I had earned a PhD degree from an Eastern University; that I had written several publications and books; it did not matter that I had traveled to Europe, Africa, and South America working for more peace and justice in our fragile global community.

Apparently, the only thing that really mattered in the worldview of this racist was the fact that I am a *black man* (the one fact I cannot change), and somehow had forgotten the old southern custom and attitude, which said: "Nigger . . . stay in your place!" Existentially, what I have discovered is that racism in America pushes your faith to the limits. But God's grace breaks the limits, and opens us up to the activity of a liberating truth. John 8:32 says: "and you will know the truth, and the truth will set you free." For Christians, truth reveals God's divine grace. It is only a glimpse into the obvious to suggest that the gift of divine grace implies—ethically—that we love God and neighbor. It is the central requirement of the covenant-harambee relationship (Matt 22:37–40; Deut.6:5cf).

Divine grace opens us up to the wonderments and love of God, despite the pains and contradictions of human existence. Joseph Sittler, a noted social ethicist, puts it nicely by saying: "the grace of God . . . is the whole giftedness of life, the wonder of life, which causes me to ask questions that transcend the moment."[25] We especially associate "wonder" in the black church tradition with the celebration of coming out of slavery: a miraculous event that involved the favor of God. Now to illustrate this sentiment and lament against slavery and systemic racism, Albert J. Raboteau, in his book *Canaan Land*, tells a passionate story about a slave named Polly and what she said to her mistress concerning God:

> We poor creatures have need to believe in God, for if God Almighty will not be good to us someday; why were we born? When I heard of his delivering his people from bondage I knew it means the poor African.[26]

The story of Exodus has held special meaning for African American Christians down through the years. Ethically, Exodus proved decisively that slavery was not only morally wrong, but contradicted the covenantal claims and promises of God (Deut 7:6–9). For people of African descent, the Exodus story became *their* story, like the Israelites of old, God had chosen them as a special people for deliverance.

In the call to worship and joyful celebration, for instance, in the contemporary black church, religious leaders, I think, must find creative ways to re-enact the trials (i.e., slavery) and triumphs (i.e., Emancipation Proclamation, Civil Rights Movement, black awareness, legacies of Mary McLeod Bethune, Rosa Parks, Coretta Scott King, etc.) of what it means to be God's chosen people in the culture of the twenty-first century. Drawing upon the biblical tradition, I suspect that African American Christians—reinforced and intensified by songs, sermons, shouts, and prayers in the context of worship—will continue to use the power of the gospel of Jesus Christ to fight against racism today. As Holy Scripture says in Galatians 3:28, "there is neither Jew nor Greek, there is neither slave nor free, there is neither male nor female; for you are all one in Christ Jesus." Therefore, a lamenting cry against racism means that it has no place in the universal *Church house* today. It has no place in the Courthouse today. It has no place in the White House today. It has no place in the "public school house" today where the contributions, cultural idioms, and values of African American children and young people are often ignored and put down by some white people. Yet there is a kind of moral resiliency inherent in the human spirit that we may all do well to remember.

To summarize this section of the chapter, it is important to say that the critical issues of AIDS, youth involvement in the total life of the Church, and racism in the wider society are enormous challenges for black leadership in the community. Of course, one of the problems peculiar to imaginative black leadership among too many African American churches today is a lack of a critical or intellectual study of the Bible. For example, Professor James Cone and other theologians have observed that, "African American preachers often draw upon biblical passages and stories in order to assist their congregants in coping with the 'hardness' of their lives . . . Preachers rely upon one or more biblical passages to provide a context for their message."[27]

What is needed is not a sugar coated message in our churches, but a hard-nose social analysis and critical thinking that empowers congregants to deal with the difficult issues of life. Therefore, the art of critical thinking about issues such as the AIDS epidemic, youth crisis, or racism, empowers the Christian believer to move from blind-faith to bold-faith in contemporary society. In short, the reality of bold-faith helps us to stand against patterns of alienation and adversity, because our confidence is grounded in Jesus Christ (Acts 4:31; 1 Tim 3:13; 2 Cor 7:4). As a people of African descent, our confidence is rooted not in the slippery slopes of *skin-color* but on the *solid rock* of Christ. To be sure, African American Christians have consistently used the Bible—through study, sermons, songs, and shouts—to bear witness to the reality of Christ in their lives. Accordingly, we shall turn, briefly, to the uses of the Bible in the black church tradition.

Uses of the Bible in Black Church Life

In the recent celebrated volume *African Americans and the Bible*, Vincent L. Wimbush, Professor of New Testament and Christian Origins at Union Theological Seminary in New York, has observed the critical importance of the biblical text in the ordinary lives of African American Christians. Informed by African *American* experience, the academic study of the Bible is different from the *pastoral* study of the Bible—in light of the perennial need to encourage congregants to struggle with the trials and tribulations in their daily lives. The Bible is a book that speaks to the majority of black people in the uneven throes of their present location, recognizing that the pains and calamities of the present location will not determine one's ultimate destination. Once you know that the Bible is more than a ritualistic manual that the church routinely presents to Sunday school children and adults then congregants can be transformed by the living word of God and triumph over adversity, sin, and oppression. Historically considered, Nathan Huggins has rightly observed: "It is essentially this triumph of the human spirit over adversity that is the great story of Afro-American slavery."[28]

Like a law book in the courthouse, the Bible was for the black slave a "deliverance book," in the "invisible institution" called the church house. Undoubtedly, the Bible is, for ordinary people of the black church tradition today, a bridge over troubled waters. Looking back, it is virtually inconceivable that the black slave would have survived without the Bible and a strong belief in the transforming word of God and stories that connected with the African American experience. Hence, we may say that "sacred texts" can speak to the pains and promise of the social context, in light of the desire on the part of the Christian believer to press toward the mark. Concerning the "uses" of the Bible in the African American experience, Professor Hans Baer asserts:

> Reverence for the Bible prompted many freed people to flock to schools set up by missionaries following the Civil War. The Bible often was a text for teaching reading skills. Many African American political activists have also used the Bible in support of their resistance to and struggle against racial oppression and economic exploitation. In the nineteenth century, these have included figures such as Denmark Vesey, Nat Turner, Harriet Tubman, and Sojourner Truth.[29]

For many African American Christians, the Bible was not only a special text for "teaching reading skills," it was also a source of instruction and guidance for the moral life. The Bible makes sense because it is the living word of God, which can inspire acts of valor and reconciliation among the wounded and marginalized in society. For Christians the world over, the Bible makes sense because it is a book that gives us an angle of vision out of which we decide issues of right and wrong, whether old or young, in our search for meaning and purpose in life. Hans Baer further argues:

The Bible often assumes a permanent presence on the pulpit as a visual reminder of its importance in the lives of the members of the congregation. In addition to enriching their sermons with biblical references, African American ministers routinely exhort their congregants to "read your Bible." Black women have played a crucial role in the creation and operation of vacation Bible schools, Bible classes, and Sunday school departments—a critical context for socialization of black children into the stories and meaning of the Bible.[30]

The Bible, in the life of the Christian community, is not merely an interesting collection of ancient stories that we may choose to embrace or discard, to like or dislike. The Bible is the redemptive story of God's grace and love for all people on the planet: the high and low, rich and poor, the haves and have-nots, the physically challenged and the gifted, and the voiceless ones in American society. Therefore, to Christian believers, the Bible is a book about us. The Bible is our communal story, but not our possession. To be sure, the Bible is a narrative book that speaks about the redeeming power and love of God, whose center is Jesus Christ, but whose witness can bear fruit for healing and reconciliation for all suffering people.

Concretely, I wish to suggest a perspective by which many people seem to use the Bible in black church life. Of course, I do not consider the following observations to be exhaustive but only suggestive for the person seeking to strengthen his or her relationship to Jesus Christ. It is Christ Jesus who saves us from our sins; it is Christ Jesus who redeems and restores the broken pieces in our lives, by the virtue of divine grace, which empowers us to understand the mystery of spiritual richness amidst the crushing poverty in the lived world of experience. Paul says: "For you know the grace of our Lord Jesus Christ, that though he was rich, yet for your sake he became poor, so that by his poverty you might become rich" (2 Cor 8:9). In my experience and/or observation:

The Bible is a Praise Book

The word *praise* originates from a Latin word meaning "value" or "price." Thus to give praise to God is to proclaim the richness of God's merit or worth. How you do this, whether you are reclining, sitting, standing, or kneeling, does not matter. All that matters is that each believer gives praise. Indeed, the human being is not only a moral agent but also a *praise-*

giving creature—as informed by the Bible. Psalms 100:4 says, "Enter his gates with thanksgiving and his courts with praise; give thanks to him and praise his name." In the life and faith of the church, the Bible has been prominently used as a source of human praise to the Divine. From a black religio-historical perspective, theologians and sociologists such as C. Eric Lincoln and E. Franklin Frazier have pointed out that the black church, as a social center of community life in the antebellum South, was originally organized as a house of praise.[31] The black church as a social institution in America began in 1773 in Silver Bluffs, South Carolina, not as a house of paupers, but as the soulful house of praise. For example, slaves were oriented to a soulful pattern of black worship down by the creek, away from the big house, where they could tell God all about their troubles! They envisioned the Bible as the normative source book of divine praise and adoration to the Triune God, who is worthy to be praised. The psalmist echoes, "Make a joyful noise to the Lord, all the earth. Worship the Lord with gladness; come into his presence with singing" (Ps 100:12).

In the corpus of the black religious experience, humor and praise have been vital parts of the Afro-American spirituals since the days of slavery. For example, the "spiritual" itself was a poetic art form of survival in regard to black oppression and the fight for freedom. As a source of survival, the slave often understood and experienced the narrative power of the spiritual in a variety of ways: "this-worldly," otherworldly, counter-cultural, contemporary, and praise-worthy. The classic spiritual or song, *"Praise Him,"* in the black church tradition illustrates this praise motif nicely:

> Praise Him
> Praise Him
> Praise Him;
> Jesus blessed Savior
> He's worthy to be praised.
>
> From the rising of the sun,
> Until the going down
> Of the same;
> Jesus blessed savior
> He's worthy to be praised.

Occasionally, the trials and tribulations in life may appear to get us down, but the *communal testimony* of the slave was that Jesus would make everything all right:

O a little talk with Jesus makes it right, all right.
Little talk with Jesus makes it right, all right.
Troubles of ev'ry kind, Thank God, I'll always find
That a little talk with Jesus makes it right.[32]

The Bible is a Book about a Prayer-Answering God

It is no accident that the Karl Barth, a renowned twentieth century theologian, advocated that all true theology begins in prayer. Many African American preachers and teachers in the black church tradition have muttered for decades such phrases as "prayer is the key to the Kingdom, and faith unlocks the door," "prayer changes things," and the profound moral dictum of Charles H. Mason, the Founder of the Church of God in Christ, once said: "I prayed earnestly that God would give me above all things a religion like the one I had heard about from the old slaves and seen demonstrated in their lives."[33]

The Bible clearly teaches us, in both the Old and New Testaments, that the Lord God delights in the prayers of the upright; and the Lord God hears the prayers of those who seek to follow righteousness (Prov 15:8, 15:29; Col 4:12; Isa 56:7). The idea of understanding a "prayer-answering-God" must not be, for the Christian believer, a mere theological proposition. Rather, at rock bottom, prayer is conversation with God. Prayer is the outpouring of one's soul, honestly and fervently, before God, before the throne of grace and mercy. After all "God made us . . . and knows all about us, better than we know ourselves," as Deacon Bush would often testify at the St. James M.B. Church, Earle, Arkansas, the religious community that nurtured my character in early childhood. For instance, my own personal narrative and faith journey reflect the power of prayer as a force that is *real* for the Christian believer. The upshot of my story, in a nutshell, is this: I wanted to go to college; my parents, though supportive of my dream did not have the money to send me to college. So I prayed, and I prayed, and I prayed again. Then God *provided a way*, seemingly out of no where vis-à-vis through a beloved uncle (Rev. Dr. Jacob C. Oglesby), gave me the money to come from Earle to Detroit to get started on the path of higher education.

Before leaving my hometown to journey to Detroit in the late summer of 1962, I remember incredible moments of adoration and praise to Almighty God for being an *Answerer* of prayer. Undoubtedly, some skeptics and secular critics may shrug their shoulders and say, "Prayer is a mere hoax . . . for the weak and non-enlightened!" But the proverbial line, "I know better," would be my testimony because of the *realness* of God's love and presence in my own life from childhood. For example, I am reminded of a gospel song, "Yes God is Real," that the choir from my home church used to sing. This poetic stanza encouraged the congregation to shout:

Yes, God is real
Yes, God is real
Real, in my soul;
For He has washed
And made me whole.

His love for me
Is like pure gold,
Yes, God is real
Yes, God is real
Real in my soul.

Now as I was packing up in 1962 to journey to Detroit—leaving behind me familiar places, faces, sounds, smells, and a joyful web of childhood experiences—I carried with me this gospel song tucked away deep within my heart. It reminded me of the *realness* of prayer as a resource in the Christian moral life. For Christian believers, the Bible teaches us that prayer is appropriate at all times, as the psalmist declared: "I call upon God . . . evening and morning and at noon I utter my complaint and moan, and he will hear my voice" (Ps 55:16–17).

In a similar vain, the psalmist cried out: "Let, I pray thee, your steadfast love become my comfort according to your promise . . . " (Ps 119:76). Of course, we as Christians are compelled to remember how prayer, as an instrument of God's steadfast love and grace, was used in the prophetic tradition (Jer 21:2, 37:20). I think we are challenged to remember that the "fervent prayers" of the righteous are affirmed by the Lord (Jas 5:16). In short, while looking back on my own tedious journey, prayer helped me to land on my feet in college. Put another way, in gratitude to Jesus Christ, "I literally prayed my way to college."

The Bible is an Inclusive Book

In the black church tradition, pastors, teachers, youth workers, and laypersons often echo a popular moral idiom, namely: "*What God's love ordained, it will maintain.*" Ethically, the word "love" obviously means different things to different people. However, there is a notion of love that is self-giving and entirely *inclusive* of the world's deepest need. John 3:16 says boldly: "For God so loved the world that he gave his only Son, so that everyone who believes in him may not perish but may have eternal life." Indeed, this *agape* love was directed—in terms of moral energy—toward the whole world, the sufferings and groanings of all humanity. Therefore, the Bible is a radically inclusive book. Metaphorically considered, the Bible is useful in the moral life of faith and struggle for "drawing circles" rather than "building walls." Here I think that the critical dialectic of faith and reason may serve to illustrate the point of biblical inclusivity.[34] As Reinhold Niebuhr, a renowned teacher of applied Christianity and social theory, often pointed out, reason is morally good as an instrument of communication and enlightenment; but it can also become a selfish servant of the will, especially the will to power. Now in the latter sense, rationalists sometimes draw circle and cut marginalized people out, but faith activists build bridges of compassion and justice, and then invite the rejected and marginalized people to *come on over the wall* and join the new community of God, without regard to gender, class, color, nationality, religion, or sexual orientation.

The Bible is a Liberation Book[35]

For people with a shared memory of suffering and oppression, the Bible is a book of hope and promise. What is hoped for by the oppressed is authentic freedom. What is promised as witnessed in the God of the Bible is deliverance. Therefore, for the sons and daughters of the *struggle* and its vicarious supporters throughout the world where suffering and injustice are daily endured, the cry for liberation is not a game, but a gift of God's liberating activity in history.

Historically, this passion for freedom inherent in the black church tradition can be poetically illustrated in the old Afro-American spiritual about the biblical character Daniel. In the story of Daniel, therefore, the slave admired the "moral guts" of Daniel himself, because he would not submit to the rule of the tyrant no matter how much power the tyrant had.[36] The song "Didn't My Lord Deliver Daniel?" echoes the majestic power of God's liberating presence:

> Didn't my Lord deliver Daniel, deliver
> Daniel, deliver Daniel,
> Didn't my Lord deliver Daniel,
> An' why not every man!
>
> He delivered Daniel f'om de lion's den,
> Jonah f'om de belly of de whale,
> De Hebrew chillum f'om de fiery furnace,
> An' why not every man![37]

For many in the black church tradition, the Bible is the universal testimony to God's liberating activity in Jesus Christ. In the final analysis, I want to strongly affirm that the Bible is a book about us—a covenant and pilgrim people of the way, who know the meaning of exile and the promise of deliverance. The Bible is a book of life-giving stories about God's relationship to us, to creation, and to the church of Jesus Christ in the world. The Bible has authority for the moral life and for Christian witness to the power of the gospel only because we believe and accept the stories of biblical faith as our stories.

As we come to the close of our reflections in this book, I strongly believe and affirm that because of the peculiar history of suffering and oppression, the endurance of the trauma of the Middle Passage on the part of people of African descent the brutality of slavery and the gallant fight for freedom—Christian ethics rooted in the black church tradition draws something significantly different from the "bucket of life" —than its white counterpart. Put another way, despite the tremendous gains made in the 1950s and 1960s by the Civil Rights Movement, African Americans and other people of color must still build coalitions, find common ground, work for justice, reconciliation, and healing of the nation—as covenant-harambee partners in the body of Christ who continue to *press toward the mark*. Nurtured in a Christian family, I grew up in the South as a child learning and singing this peculiar song that never quite escapes my moral-consciousness as a grown-up: "I'm Pressing On."

> I'm pressing on the upward way,
> New heights I am gaining
> Everyday.
> But still I am praying
> As I am onward bound
> Lord, plant my feet
> On higher ground.

Although we are fragmented beings wounded by the arrows of racism and fear in contemporary society, Christian ethics for the black church seems to call us to trust in the liberating power of the One God above our *woundedness*, who can crack open the frozen rocks of ethnic division, violence, and hatred in our world. Christian ethics for the black church today seeks an understanding of the concept of "higher ground" or "pressing on" as indicative of the love of justice and the dismantling of oppressive structures and racist attitudes of the wider society.

Theologically the search for "higher ground" is a way of affirming the revolutionary gospel of Jesus Christ, which possesses the power to shape our vision of the *inclusive* community as a people of faith—discerning the unlikely places where deep human need and human compassion meet. In the perennial moral struggle to press toward the mark, Dr. Martin Luther King, Jr., gives us a marvelous illustration on the stance of "higher ground" in his interpretation of the Good Samaritan Story:

> The Samaritan had the capacity for a universal altruism. He had a piercing insight into that which is beyond the eternal accidents of race, religion and nationality. One of the great tragedies of man's long trek along the highway of history has been the limiting of neighborly concern to tribe, race, class or nation. We see men as Jews or Gentiles, Catholics or Protestants, Chinese or American, Negroes or Whites. We fail to think of them as fellow human beings made from the same basic stuff as we, molded in the same divine image. The priest and the Levite saw only a bleeding body, not a human being like themselves. But the Good Samaritan will always remind us to remove the cataracts of provincialism from our spiritual eyes and see men as men.[38]

To be sure, the Good Samaritan story shows us both the risks of faith as well as the possibilities of faith as the church attempts to respond to human need along the Jericho road—where ordinary people of goodwill can be beaten, robbed, stripped, sexually molested, and violently abused. In the parable of the Good Samaritan, certain critical questions have to be raised about religious leaders in the community, such as What is the role of churches in relation to strangers who have been "mugged" on the Jericho Road of drugs, violence, gang war fare, racial bigotry, and the neglect of our children in contemporary society? What will happen to us if we fail to help the stranger in the community who has been "mugged" by the AIDS epidemic and often abandoned by one's immediate family? As a follower of Christ, what's in your bucket that empowers you to identify with the person "mugged," "stripped," and "beaten" by the contradictions of racism in our modern society? Ultimately, I think that the parable of the Good Samaritan raises for us not only the issue of how much *we* care about the "stranger" who is mugged and left half-beaten to death in a ditch; but how much we care about ourselves, our deepest loyalty to Christ and the cause of justice and peace in the world. To be sure, the possibilities of faith say to the Christian believer: "Don't let your momentary *potholes* determine God's promises in your life, as you press toward the mark."

Accordingly, for many people embracing the Good Samaritan spirit, what will happen to us as a nation, if we fail to know, remember, and internalize the legacies of Mary McLeod Bethune, Rosa Parks, Coretta Scott King and countless others of the black church tradition who dared to believe that it is more important to light the *candle of freedom* than to curse the darkness of *unfreedom*?

Accordingly, I wish to conclude our discussion in this book by outlining, briefly, twelve-ethical marks or moral laws that may be helpful as we face God's future for our lives. As a teaching resource, I have intentionally set up each chapter of the book to end with a case study. Therefore, write down and discuss your feelings about the case and its ethical implications.

Twelve Moral Laws for Pressing Toward the Mark

As we attempt to press toward the mark in both church and society, I wish you would consider this bone-dry outline that may assist all of us along the way of our moral and spiritual journey in life. Walter G. Muelder, in his classic book *Moral Law in Christian Social Ethics*, provides the reader with a keen insight into the nature of moral laws. Logically, we start as Christian believers with the ethical question, "What are moral laws?"[39] Briefly and functionally considered, I find it compelling that Muelder defines moral laws as "normative laws of choice. They are the principles of responsible decision . . . and any guideline principle for action *ought* to be consistent and coherent with the proposed system of moral laws.[40]

In a nutshell, "moral laws" are expressive of the *covenant-harambee* model for practicing Christian ethics in the black church tradition. The central features of the *covenant-harambee* approach, I think, must necessarily include the importance of "social solidarity," "unity," "faith," "love of justice," "familihood," "cooperative economics," "quality education," and a safe environment for the moral growth and development of our children in the community. The "moral laws" of covenant-harambee must be the wave of the future if we are to have a sustainable and prosperous future in American society. Covenant-harambee, as we have already discussed, literally means *putting together*. Either we pull together or we pull-*apart*! Covenant-harambee signals both "obligations" and "blessings," on the part of the Christian believer. Existentially, it means that God got a blessing with your name on it (Deut 28:8; Ps 129:8; Prov 10:22, 24:25). It means that this is your day—so just reach out and claim the "blessing" by faith.

Notwithstanding, the covenant-harambee approach to doing ethics in the black church tradition acknowledges that every individual will, undoubtedly, have some "bumps" along the road of life. Yet the reality of covenant-harambee means that God can change your "bumps" into "blessings." The covenant-harambee approach in the Christian moral life seeks to respond to the needs of every child with a caring adult who can provide protection, guidance, support, and spiritual direction in the church community. To be sure, the "moral laws" implicit in the covenant-harambee model reflect a breaking-away from the old paradigm of possessive individualism—which boast arrogantly: " . . . *my* resources and *my* money . . . *my* family and *my* fortune . . . *my* child and her stuff." By contrast, we must have the courage to articulate a new paradigm on the part of the Christian believer—where parents, relatives, and adult caretakers can boldly say: "These are *our* children . . . whether homeless or sheltered . . . in need of love and nurture in our neighborhoods. These are *our* neglected youth and adolescents . . . in need of a hug, a warm embrace, encouragement, positive role models, and the church's outreach against the raging tide of violence and hopelessness in far too many places in urban America." Indeed, the "moral laws" reflected in the covenant-harambee model just may remind the ordinary person of faith the wisdom of the African proverb: "*It Takes a Village to Raise a Child.*" Concretely, moral laws challenge each individual believer or follower of Christ to embrace and uphold certain principles that speak to particular decisions in particular situations. For example, many people who participated in the Civil Rights movement in the sixties advocated principles like freedom, justice, equality, love, forgiveness, and reconciliation in our common life. For African Americans, the composite experiences of pain and suffering have everything to do with the "normative laws of choice." I strongly affirm and believe that the reality of *choice* is at the heart of the Christian moral life. To be sure, we as moral agents can choose to serve God or not to serve God (Josh 24:15); we can choose to follow Christ or not. We may choose to press toward the mark or remain where we are. In short, we may choose what moral laws or principles we put in our *buckets*, in order to be happy, successful, and faithful to God.

In summary, Christian ethics in regard to black church tradition may include the following "moral laws" or *proverbial principles* by which we can live a better life in American society—despite the nagging problems of racism, sexism, classism, AIDS, youth identity, and crass materialism that so easily effect us all. As a largely Bible-centered people, I have chosen the number *twelve*—symbolically—in regard to "moral laws" because Jesus had 12 original disciples. Therefore, be not ashamed to put these *prover-bial principles* in your bucket:

1. Live life, love life, serve life. (See Deut 30:19–25; Josh 10:10; Matt 20:26)

2. Do not trust another individual to do for you, what you alone can do for yourself. (See Ps 37:1–7; Prov 2:1–10)

3. Thank God for making you the way you are: unique and beautiful—like none other—as a child of God. (See Ps 2:4–9; Acts 8:26–38)

4. Remember always that "black history" did not begin with slavery, but with ancient Egyptian kings, queens, scientists, sages, and arti-sans of Mother Africa. (See Matt 2:15; 1 Pet 2:9–10)

5. Faith is to freedom what Civil Rights is to the oppressed around the world. (See Deut 7:7–11; Isa 61:1–4)

6. Faith is to freedom what the "underground railroad" was to the ex-slave. (See Exod 20:1–5, 23:1–9; Gal 5:1)

7. Faith never says, "three strikes and you're out!" but, "*one surrender* to Christ and you're in!" (See Heb 11:1–11; Jas 1:2–4)

8. There can be no *healing* of the nation, without *forgiveness* in the human heart. (See Matt 11:26; Luke 6:37)

9. Do what you can to make a difference, and let it go. (See Mic 6:8; Ps 19:7–11)

10. Throw down ropes from the mountain of success rather than scis-sors, so others—black or white—may be able to climb. (See Gal 6:2; Matt 25:35)

11. Freedom without self-responsibility is self-deception. (See Eph 6:11; Gal 6:5)

12. Let justice be done, though the heavens fall; follow Jesus today as your all and all. (See Mic 3:8; Matt 12:18)

Case Study: Turn It Over to God

"I felt angry, bitter, and ashamed when I was told that my job had been phased out as a result of a reorganization plan," explained Steve Long, a 35-year-old ex-banker who is currently serving as interim pastor of the Mt. Olive Baptist Church, St. Louis, Missouri. In terms of family life, he is married to Beverly Long and they are the proud parents of two children,

Erin, age 10, and Theresa, age 7. But life for the Long family has not been a crystal stair. Indeed, his road to the pathway of Christian ministry has often been paved with bumps along the way. Let us now try and put part of his life story into perspective, as we examine certain aspects of his case history and struggle.

Steve Long has been active in some form of Christian service since his agonizing decision to accept the "call" to the ministry back in 1997. His spiritual director or mentor was an energetic country preacher from Georgia who bore the name, "the son of thunder," the Rev. A. P. Perry. The church family of his childhood was the Pine Grove Baptist Church of Sornoraville, Georgia. The community of Sornoraville was also his place of birth. Now under Rev. Perry's strong preaching and spiritual leadership, Steve Long's own identity was shaped in the direction of the Christian ministry. Regarding human struggle, Rev. Perry would characteristically end his Sunday morning sermons with this spiritual refrain: "Oh children, whatever the pain, whatever the problem . . . take your burdens to the Lord and leave them there . . . *turn it over to God.*"

These words seemingly formed a resounding echo in the heart of Steve Long as he came face to face with his own feelings of hurt over losing his job as a banker—a job that provided economic security in sustaining his middle class lifestyle. But now the boundaries of his social situation had changed. His fear and anxiety were real; for the loss of employment income also meant a loss of social status, buying power, and esteem. Yet he reasoned within himself that, "whatever the problem, the Lord God would make a way out of no way, and see me through." Although he felt sometimes lonely and frustrated, he still believed that God was somehow involved in his day-to-day struggle. Come what may, Steve apparently felt that he was not going to let go of his religion, or get angry with God about his job situation. It would seem in the interview that the opposite was the case: rather than blame God for his situation, he found courage and inward strength to *turn it over to God*. In some respects, the gravity of his job crisis actually functioned to draw him closer to the Divine, and into the realm of God's sustaining presence. The terrible sting of joblessness is often, psychologically, severe enough to make the average person "curse God and die," but not so in the faith story and struggles of Steve Long. In this case, his religious faith became apparently stronger because of his personal crisis. Religious faith, apparently, became the cement that held his shattered life together. In his own life story, we may observe that an informing source was his grandmother. In his extended family, she represented a tower of strength. As grandmother, she stubbornly insisted that the young ones could do well in life, only if they kept Jesus and "old time religion" close to their bosom. Her favorable admonition to them was taken from an old Negro spiritual that read:

> I ain't gwine to lay my 'ligion down,
> I ain't gwine to lay my 'ligion down,
> Children, I ain't gwine lay my 'ligion down.

For Steve Long, this spontaneous expression growing out of the well-spring of black religious experience pointed the human spirit toward God, and away from the long bitter night of joblessness and disappointment. For Steve, the main locus of his grandmother's urging which impacted his character was not that "religion" per se would provide an ideal new job for him—if only one prays three times a day—but rather religion is like a living fountain which sustains the individual person through good times and bad times. In his way of thinking, religious faith becomes a sword which enables the believer to do battle against injustices and the "principalities and powers" by putting on the "whole armor of God." The phrase "I ain't gwine lay my 'ligion down" actually symbolized for Steve Long a peculiar way of keeping faith in the midst of a despairing situation. It was a way of turning a situation of despair into a situation of hope. For all of us, this is easier said than done. In any event, the real struggle for Steve centers in the way we understand faith itself. I asked him: "What are your feelings about the meaning of faith?" He briskly responded: "I feel that true faith is not something that you can simply define by going to a dictionary or theological handbook . . . it is more than that. All through life, I think that I have been exposed to somewhat of a 'head definition' of faith and not a heart definition. What I mean to be saying is . . . when your heart is bleeding because you find yourself out of work; that turns your whole life upside down. Sometimes you just feel like hiding because your heart is heavy, you feel burdened down; and at that point, everything that you have been taught in your head about faith makes no sense. I have found that true faith helps you to work through what you feel in your heart." "Well, Steve, what do you feel in your heart right now about your situation," I asked? He replied: "I still feel uneasy about the future and my whole job situation . . . I have had lots of good interviews but the banking industry is in transition, and it may be hard to find full time employment at the level I was functioning. What is often frustrating when you go for a job interview is that you are either over qualified with too much work experience, or they tell you to wait a few months and you discover, surprisingly, that the job was given to someone else . . . then you feel all angry and mixed-up inside

. . . Here, true faith of the 'heart' means accepting the future, not knowing what it holds."

Now a closer look at Steve Long's own story revealed that he is a responsible and religiously mature person who has been in the banking industry for over five years. He has a good work record with a major banking institution. His professional profile would suggest a person of competency, loyalty, and cooperation. Indeed, the spirit of cooperation would best describe his social conduct in the work-a-day world. Much of who he is as an adult stems from his "down-home" attitude and training in the small rural community of Sornoraville, Georgia. With a population of less than 200 people, everybody in the community had a sense of family belonging. Ben and Alice Long, the parents of Steve, were hardworking people who had seasonal responsibility for cultivating 162 acres of farmland. So early in life, young Steve gained an appreciation for the values of discipline and work. Like most African Americans, the Long family regarded education as a high value of worth. For example, Steve graduated from his local high school with honors. He then went on to attend Morehouse College in Atlanta and eventually graduated in the early 1990s with a degree in business. Recalling a few difficulties during his period of college life, Steve remarked, "I found the academic side of college life most challenging, largely because I had to compete with students who were the sons of doctors and lawyers . . . but I said to myself . . . 'I am on my own, I can make it; I can do it . . . with God's help, I can succeed.'" Further, we may observe that soon after graduation from college, an important turning point took place in the life and faith pilgrimage of Steve Long. Here he, apparently, struggled many sleepless nights with the decision to go to seminary in preparation for Christian ministry. Accordingly, Steve pursued the goal of a theological education by enrolling at the Interdenominational Theological Center of Atlanta. But because of job and family pressures at the time, he found it difficult to successfully coordinate the increasing demands of school and full-time employment. Steve recalled the gravity of his emerging dilemma in these words: "I really had too many irons in the fire at that time. I had a family, a new job, and church responsibilities . . . so my studies at the seminary were pushed on the back burner. I found myself terribly distracted and frustrated over many things . . . eventually, we just left Atlanta and moved to Memphis. There, I joined a Unitarian Universalistic Church for a while, but that was short-lived. Looking back, it's really strange because there I didn't feel that I was in touch with either my calling or the God of the Bible which I had learned about from my grandmother as a child . . . It was a way-out phase I went through before coming to St. Louis in the mid-1990s."

Summarily, the fact of the matter is that the actual shape of Steve's own personal faith has taken on a new form since his recent struggle over his job situation. He suggested to me that his own struggle and pain of being laid off had deepened his sense of faith and dedication to the work and ministry of the church of Jesus Christ, at least two levels. The first level is that of lifestyle and social expectation. Here Steve Long and his family appear to be rethinking, in a different light, the enormous importance our culture seems to attach to material success, as the sole definition of well-being and happiness in life. Of course, he would not go so far as to call his crisis of employment as a "blessing in disguise," but there was, nonetheless, a strong indication that a more simplified material lifestyle was a move in the right direction for middle class black Americans. Thus in the life story of Steve Long, there was a strong feeling that the gospel of Jesus Christ calls us to affirm that each person's worth is more than the sum total of one's possessions. The second level of change I observed had to do with a deepening of faith. Here there was the feeling expressed that the realities of anger and loss resulting from his job situation, actually functioned to renew faith and commitment to God. Steve used these words to describe this second level: "Really, I discovered that out of my suffering . . . my own understanding of faith itself was being changed; my feelings about myself were changing also . . . Now, I am painfully learning not so much how to try and control my life or the future, but just to accept what is presented; strangely, I find myself praying more . . . and turning things over to God more; it is as simple and difficult as that . . . . " As a morally sensitive person one can, no doubt, feel the pull and struggle and the tension and hope in these words. There is a reaching up for more strength; there is a downward anchoring for more courage; and there is the inward struggle of faith to make sense out of our own suffering and shifting circumstance. Perhaps it is more important to say that at the close of the interview we may observe that the boundaries of Steve Long's external circumstances have not really changed: he is still without regular employment, and that of course bothers him; but what has changed is the internal landscape, the manner in which he has chosen to respond. For Steve, the God inside of him seems to give strength for the next step, although he is not sure what that next step will be.

A Brief Note

I wish to provide the reader with a brief note, because this case is a bit longer than previous ones. This case involves the problems and difficulties experienced by a middle class Christian, who suddenly finds himself laid off from a good paying job in the banking industry. The feelings of bitterness and embarrassment often fester in the hearts of those in similar situations as Steve Long. In the consumer culture of our contemporary society the individual person seems to derive social identity and value largely from one's occupational status or economic stratum. Education, competition, and competency are prevailing values of the marketplace, which tend to influence the choices we make as well as the lifestyles we lead. Accordingly, some would say that to be without a job, to be unemployed in our consumer culture is tantamount to social treason and a loss of identity.

For the morally sensitive Christian, the story of Steve seems to suggest an alternative view of social reality—despite the prevailing norms and values of our consumer culture. It seems to me that one of the issues, which this case opens, is the power of faith in a personal God in the midst of "bad times" as well as good times. Does God care about my own situation of unemployment and personal anguish? Can I trust God when my back is against the wall of joblessness? Will God answer me and deliver me from my present crisis? As a community of faith, can we trust God to see us through the storms of life?

These are vital questions to keep on the front burner of the black religious community in America. Notwithstanding, given the current social economic climate of African Americans today, recent studies suggest that the median weekly wage earned by blacks in 2004 was $425; for white workers, it was $677 a week. One out of four (25.7 percent) African Americans is employed as a nursing or home healthcare worker, cook, janitor, maid, cashier, salesperson, customer service representative, secretary, truck driver, or laborer. Annual salaries for these professions range from $29,020 to $10,335.

Comparatively, the unemployment rate for black people living in America is twice that for whites. Moreover, employment rates continue to be higher for white youth, at 62 percent, than for African American youth, at 42 percent. It is ethically outrageous that African Americans today have only a median net worth of $5,998 compared to $88,651 for whites. Even more alarming, 32 percent of African Americans have a zero or negative net worth. Although African Americans are more than 13 percent of the nation's population, their total net worth is only 1.2 percent of the total net worth of the nation. This number has not changed since the end of the Civil War in 1865. Fewer than 50 percent actually own their own homes, compared with more than 75 percent of whites. African Americans are 3.6 times as likely as whites to receive a home purchase loan from a sub-prime lender and 4.1 times as likely as whites to receive a refinance loan from a sub-prime lender. Hence, sub-prime lending is usually 1 to 6 points over the prime rate. It is only a glimpse into the obvious to suggest that this disparity puts potential black homeowners at a profound moral disadvantage. Now the bottom line of this scenario, in regard to the case study of Steve Long, would strongly suggest that job layoffs in the banking industry is a systemic problem for blacks and other people of color (See Tavis Smiley, ed., *The Covenant*, Chicago: Third World Press, 2006, 110–170).

Ethically, it is my strong conviction that the greatest challenge confronting African American believers today emanates not only from critical issues raised in this book, but also the challenge to reclaim and refine what Professor Henry H. Mitchell called "the spirit . . . that uplifted so many illiterate ex-slaves, built schools for them, briefly shaped government for them, and encouraged the newly freed as they launched out into the deep of private enterprise." As we continue to struggle in pressing toward the mark in the contemporary black church, Mitchell rightly reminds us, I think, that "the starting place is in the resurrection of our own self-image, to look at our great-great grandparents and rediscover who we really are, and what in fact is our potential." (See Henry H. Mitchell, *Black Church Beginnings*, Grand Rapids: William B. Eerdmans Publishing Co., 2004, p. 181).

Ethical Approach

1. How would you likely respond to Steve Long's dilemma?

2. Does he appear to have feelings of anger, shame or self-doubt?

3. Is there any distinctive element or advantage to a "Christian approach" in dealing with the tension of job loss?

4. What "moral laws" must be in the *bucket* of the contemporary black church in order to deal with the messy problems of AIDS, racism, sexism, and youth estrangement in our society today?

Issues for Study and Discussion

1. What do you think of the way Steve Long reacted to being laid-off his job as a banker? (See Prov 4:1–7)

2. What issues of lifestyle or "social identity" are raised by this case? (See Ps 8:4–9, 4:1–8)

3. Should morally sensitive persons be suspicious when corporations or institutions use such language as "reorganization plan"? (See Mic 2:1–2; Jer 5:26–29)

4. What is the "faithful thing to do" as a follower of Christ? (See Matt 6:33; Heb 11:1)

5. What sort of values or principles should Steve have in his *bucket*? (See Mic 6:8; Matt 22:37–40)

6. Are there issues of racial injustice implied in this case? If so, please illustrate. (See Acts 11:1–18).

Notes

1. Tom Rath and Donald O. Clifton, *How Full is Your Bucket?* (New York: Gallup Press, 2004) 24–26. For the student of Christian ethics—either in African American churches or Eurocentric churches—the insights in this volume are enormously helpful in struggling with issues of identity, self-esteem, faith, and the psychology of positive thinking. On the back cover, Martin Walsh, Executive Director of the Society for Human Resource Management (SHRM), has made the following comment concerning this provocative book: "Wow! This . . . book is a treasure. It is chock full of wisdom, inspiration, and practical advice, rooted in solid research. It will change the way you look at your life, your work, and your world." For Christians, these authors seem to raise for us not some simple psychological theory of positive thinking, negating ambiguity and the torture of racial injustice; rather it invites the reader to use constructive positive thinking *and* faith to grapple with the difficulties of life in America.

2. Ibid., 15.

3. Ibid.

4. Joseph L. Allen, *Love and Conflict: A Covenantal Model of Christian Ethics* (Nashville: Abingdon Press, 1984) 15. As an ethicist, Allen elaborates upon the typology of covenant, which includes two essential forms: inclusive and exclusive. Broadly, he articulates a theory of covenant—biblically grounded—around the relational concept of *entrustment*, with varying motifs of interpretation depending on the community of faith and social context. For example, the commandment, "Love thy neighbor as thyself" is the strongest expression of what may be called the *inclusive covenant*, binding upon all humanity. Whereas the covenant of marriage, for example, falls under the theoretical category of the *exclusive covenant*, in the critical thought and writings of Allen.

5. Ibid., 32.

6. Ibid.

7. John Lovell, Jr., *Black Song: The Forge and the Flame* (New York: Paragon House Publishers, 1972) 231. Religious scholars and social historians alike agree that music has played a shaping role in the black church tradition, especially our study and fascination of the Afro-American spiritual. *Black Song* is the kind of dynamic book that discusses the powerful influence of spirituals on different forms of modern music, culture, character formation, and black church life in society today. For Lovell, the Afro-American spiritual has the capacity to transcend race, color, class, or gender—because its art form has a universal appeal to the human heart. There is a blending of both prophetic imagination and poetic imagination inherent in the experiences of spirituals on the part of the listener or moral agent. I find it compelling for the reader to note that Lovell carefully identifies at least seven functions or purposes of the Afro-American spiritual: (*a*) "to give the community a true, valid and useful song; (*b*) to keep the community invigorated; (*c*) to inspire the uninspired individual; (*d*) to enable the group to face its problems; (*e*) to comment on the slave situation; (*f*) to stir each member to personal solutions . . . in the midst of a confusing and terrifying world; and (*g*) to provide a code of language for emergency use," 198.

8. E. Hammond Oglesby, *O Lord, Move This Mountain: Racism and Christian Ethics* (St. Louis: Chalice Press, 1998) 55–69.

9. E. Hammond Oglesby, *Ethical Issues That Matter: A New Method of Moral Discourse in Church Life* (Lanham, Maryland: University Press of America, Inc., 2002) 71.

10. Maulana Karenga, *Kwanzaa: A Celebration of Family, Community, and Culture* (Los Angeles: University of San Kore Press, 1998) 34, 96 cf.

11. Oglesby, *Ethical Issues That Matter*, 72.

12. Ibid., 132.

13. Ibid.

14. Kenneth R. Overberg, ed., *Aids, Ethics and Religion: Embracing a World of Suffering* (Maryknoll, New York: Orbis Press, 1994) 5.

15. Jonathan M. Ellen, M.D., "*The Hopkins HIV Report*" (John Hopkins AIDS Service: May, 2002) 3–6. Dr. Ellen focuses his research analysis on adolescents and HIV patients and the kinds of lifestyle behavior that typically charactizes the stage of adolescence. Once considered by many social critics as a white epidemic in the United States, AIDS has now changed color. Accordingly, the data suggest that racial/ethnic minorities are now at the greater risk. Dr. Ellen has observed that, "Adolescent health care providers in geographic regions hard hit by HIV are now faced with two important trends. First, a large cohort of youth infected by birth and sustained by Highly Active Antiretroviral Treatment (HAART) is coming of age and in need of specialized medical care . . . . Secondly, unaffected youth are entering a phase of their lives in which their behavior choices . . . could dramatically increase their risk of HIV infection," 2–6.

16. William J. Cromie, "AIDS Epidemic Called Crisis Among Blacks" (*The Harvard University Gazette*: March 19, 1998) 1.

17. Ibid., 1–2.

18. Ibid.

19. Ibid., 2–3 cf.

20. Steven J. Goodwin, ed., *AIDS Reference Guide: A Source Book for Planners and Decision Makers* (Washington, D.C.: Atlantic Information Services, Inc., 2000) 3.

21. Oglesby, *Ethical Issues That Matter*, 104.

22. Calvin Thomas III, "*An Ecclesial Response: The Young African American Male Exodus*" (St. Louis: Eden Theological Seminary, Calvin Thomas' unpublished Master's Thesis, Spring, 2006) 25.

23. Ibid., 24-26.

24. Joseph Barndt, *Dismantling Racism: The Continuing Challenge to White America* (Minneapolis: Augsburg Fortress, 1991) 28 cf.

25. William K. McElvaney, *Winds of Grace, Ways of Faith* (Louisville: Westminster/ John Knox Press, 1991) 49.

26. Albert J. Raboteau, *Canaan Land: A Religious History of African Americans* (New York: Oxford University Press, 2001) 44.

27. Vincent L. Wimbush, ed., *African Americans and the Bible: Sacred Tests and Social Textures* (New York: Continuum International Publishing Group, Inc., 2000) 75.

28. Richard Newman, *African American Quotations* (New York: Checkmark Books, 2000) 326.

29. Cited in Wimbush, ed., 75.

30. Ibid.

31. E. Hammond Oglesby, *Ten Principles of Black Self-Esteem: Letters of Heritages, Lessons of Hope* (Cleveland: The Pilgrim Press, 1999) 101.

32. Lovell, 318.

33 Newman, 285.

34. Oglesby, *Ten Principles of Black Self-Esteem*, 102cf.

35. Ibid., 103.

36. Lovell, 329 cf.

37. Ibid.

38. Cited in Preston Robert Washington, *God's Transforming Spirit: Black Church Renewal* (Valley Forge: Judson Press, 1988) 137.

39. Walter G. Muelder, *Moral Law in Christian Social Ethics* (Richmond, Virginia: John Knox Press, 1966) 11–23.

40. Ibid., 10.